"The One Page Business Plan
does something outrageous!
It causes very busy people
to stop and think.
As they start to write...
it confirms both their clarity
and their confusion!"

— **Jim Horan**
President
The One Page Business Plan Company

DISCLAIMER

This book was designed to provide information in regard to the subject matter covered. It is not the purpose of this manual to reprint all of the information available to the author/publisher, but to complement, amplify and supplement other sources.

Use of The One Page Business Plan® does not in any way guarantee the success of an idea or organization, nor does it ensure that financing will be made available. When legal or expert assistance is required, the services of a competent professional should be sought.

The author/publisher shall have neither liability nor responsibility to any person or entity with respect to any loss or damage caused, or alleged to be caused, directly or indirectly by the information contained in this book.

If you do not wish to be bound by the above, you may return this book to the publisher for a full refund.

Published by:

The One Page Business Plan Company
www.onepagebusinessplan.com

ISBN: 9781797571744

6th EDITION

Book Design by: Melodie Bacon
Cover design by: Joni McPherson

Printed in the United States of America v1.0

The One Page Business Plan®

*The Fastest, Easiest Way
to Write a Business Plan!*

By Jim Horan

Professional Consultant Edition

Foreword

What Others Are Saying

The One Page Business Plan® *takes a complex process and makes it simple!*

This is a friendly, but no nonsense approach to business planning that got me over my reluctance to write a business plan. This process got me to think out of the box! And to actually get my plan written! One Page Plans rock!
Kendall Moalem, Kendall Moalem Design & Consulting

As a business owner and consultant, I've had a number of business plans, but none of them were effective. Having all the essentials of our plan on one page helped get me and my consulting partners get and stay on track!
Norman Kurtin, Master Instructional Designer, Re: Mind

I had been writing the same goals and visions for my business over and over. What I wrote in March, I wrote in June, and again in September. After I heard Jim speak, I wrote my one page plan. I now choose my opportunities more wisely and waste less time because I have my plan in place.
Linda Pollock, Professional Organizer

The One Page Business Plan truly helps the prospective entrepreneur or existing business owner get focused and clear on one page. When they are clear on one page, they have a much better chance for success! As a consultant, I now have a One Page Plan, and I am much more focused and clear.
Greg Garrett, Consultant & Program Manager, One Stop Capital Shop

It's easy for a stockbroker to get wrapped up in the market and lose perspective that you are in business for yourself. In order to be successful for the long run, one must have a plan and The One Page Business Plan is a great tool.
Ralph Miljanich, Sr. Financial Advisor/Consultant, Vice President, Morgan Stanley, Inc.

The One Page Business Plan is the business plan for independent professionals. It de-mystifies business planning so that the average business professional can actually write a business plan that makes sense!
Rebecca Salome, Entrepreneurial Authors

Jim's presentation on The One Page Business Plan was absolutely enlightening! I finally realized that as a therapist, I am an entrepreneur and a business owner. I now have a business plan that is helping me build my practice.
Mia Salaverry, MFCC

I quickly glanced at The One Page Business Plan format and knew it was what I was looking for. Within a couple of hours, I had my first draft. Now I have a business plan that I really understand.
Norman Meshriy, Career Insights, author of "Outside the Cubicle".

I've written the long business plans more than once and they sat gathering dust. They were too involved to help me stay on track. The One Page Business Plan makes planning doable, flexible, and usable.
Elaine Groen R.D., Nutrition Source

I recommend The One Page Business Plan to anyone wanting to free themselves from the fear and terror of writing a business plan. Jim's book is totally user-friendly, highly efficient, and best of all fun.
Jan St. John, Founder of 21st Century Radio Production

"*You must simplify. You must make the complex simple, then you must make it work.*"

— I.M. Pei
Master Architect

About Jim Horan

As an author, speaker, and consultant, Jim Horan had the unique ability to take complex business situations and make them simple. The One Page Business Plan for the Creative Entrepreneur was first published in 1997 and quickly became an Amazon.com best-seller. Since then, Jim added six more editions of the book for various industries including non-profits, corporate executives, financial services and consultants. In addition, the original book has been translated into four different languages.

Jim deeply cared about people, the environment, and their communities. In 1990, after spending 17 years in Fortune 500 companies as a senior financial executive, he found himself unemployed and decided to start his own business. As an entrepreneur himself, Jim was drawn to working with other entrepreneurs and independent business owners. With that work in mind, he was inspired to create an innovative, fresh approach to business planning designed to act as a repository for the planner's best thinking. It quickly became a powerful tool for building and managing a business. Jim's short, concise methods quickly get the reader's ideas out of their head and on to paper.

Today, The One Page Business Plan Company is a broad-based, global consulting company serving entrepreneurs, Fortune 500 executives and business owners in a wide range of industries. Over the past 25 years, this company has helped over a quarter million businesses achieve more sustainable cash flow and profitable growth... including companies like Oracle, IKON Office Systems, Guardian Life Insurance, Morgan Stanley, Northwestern Mutual Financial Network, The Principal, Northrup Grumman, Herman-Miller, YWCA & YMCA, The Ken Blanchard Companies and Tillamook Cheese.

Jim Horan passed away unexpectedly on September 19, 2019, but not before he had helped thousands of entrepreneurs, business owners, and senior executives clarify their own paths forward. Here at the One Page Business Plan Company, we are dedicated to continuing on with Jim's vision and legacy, celebrating his breakthrough thinking of the past 25 years... so his ideas will continue to inspire millions more to build better businesses and non-profit organizations.

How to Use This Book and eToolkit

The primary purpose of this book is to help you get your plan onto paper. It has been carefully crafted to capture the plan that is in your head.

Carry this book with you, write in it, use it as a container for capturing your thoughts as they occur. If you have multiple businesses, partners or managers, have them get their own copy.

It's not necessary to do all the exercises in this book. If you can write your One Page Business Plan by reviewing the samples — skip the exercises. They are there to help guide you through the process if you need help.

This book does not look like the typical business planning book — it isn't intended to. The exercises and examples are meant to stimulate you. The graphics and images are meant to guide you. If they look playful, be playful and explore. If they look analytical, be analytical and focused. The examples and samples are from real business plans. They are meant to show you how powerful a few words or a well-constructed phrase can be.

Do not underestimate the power of the questions that appear simple! They are simple by design. If you do not get an "aha" from them, have somebody ask you the questions. Important insights may begin to flow.

This book is divided into nine sections with the focus on the five elements of The One Page Business Plan. You can start anywhere. It's OK to jump around!

There are many different ways to use and interact with this book. Exercises can be done:

- by oneself

- with a planning partner (2 or more consultants)

- as a management team

- as a group

- with a paid advisor

The Consultant's eToolkit (download link on the last page of the book) contains the One Page Business Plan templates, bonus exercises, One Page budget worksheet, plus Scorecards for monitoring and tracking your results.

It also contains several articles on critical sales and marketing best practices you must master in order to build a successful consulting practice!

Business Plan Myths

- All business plans are in writing.

- They must be long to be good.

- Their primary purpose is to obtain financing.

- It's easier for others to write business plans.

- You can and should do it by yourself.

- It takes six months, a significant amount of executive and staff's time, and expensive consultants.

- If completed, it will sit unused on a bookshelf.

- My practice is too small; business plans are for much bigger organizations.

- I know where I am taking my business; I do not need a written business plan.

- I can just pay for a consultant to write the plan for me; that will be good enough.

Let's dispel the myths...

Table of Contents

ONLINE SYSTEM: The One Page Business Plan is MORE Than Just a Book!

This Book Was Just the Beginning....

Our One Page Planning and Performance System takes the best of The One Page Business Plan ® process to create a powerful strategic and tactical, real-world performance management online system that helps mid-sized companies:

• Accelerate growth
• Develop stronger communication between divisions
• Cascade your strategic decisions throughout your organization
• Focus people and resources on achieving company goals
• Develop high performance leaders
• Find and hold your focus on what's important all year long

It's a proven online tool that uniquely links planning, strategy, performance, and accountability. It's simple, it's easy and it works!

Curious? Take a free tour of the system at www.onepagebusinessplan.com

ONE PAGE PLANS
Click on any business unit to see a One Page Plan.

ONE PAGE PROGRESS REPORTS
Click on any Plan to view One Page Progress Reports.

ONE PAGE SCORECARDS
Click on any Objective to view One Page Performance Scorecards.

The One Page Business Plan Company has grown over the past 25 years into an international consulting firm with over 500 licensed consultants worldwide. Our company is recognized as a leader with its innovative cloud-based planning and performance management systems.

Introduction

What is a One Page Business Plan?

"Planning is a process... not an event!

One Page Plans are living, changing, evolving documents!"

The One Page Business Plan is an innovative approach to business planning that captures the essence of any business, project or program on a single page using key words and short phrases.

Most companies use the process to create not only the company's overall plan, but to create a plan for each supporting department, project and program. Since the creation of The One Page Business Plan in 1994, over 500,000 companies have successfully used the process to bring structure, alignment and accountability to their organizations. Many of those companies were professional services firms.

The flexible methodology makes it possible for entrepreneurs, business owners, executives, managers and professionals in any organization to each have a plan. The standard format makes it easy to review, compare and understand plans.

One Page Business Plans work because:

- Plans actually get documented
- Plans are understandable
- Plans are easy to write, easy to update
- Every manager or team has one

The process creates:

- Alignment
- Accountability
- Results

Our Observations...

Why One Page?

You are busy; your time is limited. You want to spend your time being billable. Creating products and services. Marketing and selling your services. You are action and results oriented. Most of us are not good at prose writing... it takes too long to write a well-written sentence, paragraph, page or chapter. And far too long to read. People need to be able to read a plan in about five minutes. They want the essence... the key points. Then they want to talk... to ask clarifying questions, come to agreement... and then take action.

Why Plan?

Some need to write plans to get funding... however since few consulting practices are fundable other than by friends and family, funding is not the primary reason consultants write plans. Most people write plans because they either want or need to achieve different or better results. Plans are blueprints; they describe what is going to be built, how it will be done, and by whom... and the results to be measured.

Why Written Plans?

The spoken word is too fluid; we have a tendency to ramble. When we speak we almost never say it exactly the same way... frequently we forget to share some of the most important details... or spend too much time on the unimportant things. When we write, we choose our words more carefully. Writing takes time, usually much more than talk. The written word requires a higher level of mindfulness and attention to detail. The written word also produces a contract with yourself and others that can be reread, refined... a source for refection and mindful change if necessary.

Asking people simple questions... works!

People love to talk about their business! They can easily answer questions like, what are you building, what will your practice look like in three years, what has made your consulting business successful to date, what are the critical practice development projects and programs you have underway or planned, what do you measure to know if you are on track... and of course, why does your business exist?

The Power is in 5 Key Questions!

Business plan terminology is problematic. Depending on where you went to school, and the companies/organizations you have worked for... the terms Vision, Mission, Objectives, Strategies and Plans probably mean something different to you than the person sitting next to you. We have learned that business planning "definitions" just don't work. We have refined our questions over twelve years with thousands of business owners. The five questions we will teach you are simple, easy to remember and they will help get your business plan out of your head and onto paper.

About Planning Processes

Starting with a blank page wastes valuable time!

The examples and the fill-in-the-blank prompts are learning aids... designed to help you learn and master the One Page Business Plan technique quickly. We have learned that most people learn by seeing examples, so we give you lots of them.

The dreaded "writer's block" can easily be eliminated by the use of our proprietary fill-in-the-blank templates. They make the creation of any portion of your business plan easy. Use the fill-in-the-blank templates to quickly capture your thoughts and create the first draft. You will also find that the extensive list of templates can spark your thinking and make sure that you are concerned with your "total" business.

Everyone on your team can and should write a One Page Business Plan!

The number one issue business owners and executives share with us is that they need people to work on the right things... and achieve specific results! Partners complain they are not on the same page! There is a simple solution: have your partners, associates, strategic alliance partner, managers and paid staff create One Page Business Plans for their businesses, profit centers, departments, projects or programs. Do not assume they are executing your plan. Have them create their own!

Final Thought: Plans are important... Execution is critical!

Consulting companies invest in planning because they want and need results. Plans are valuable because they provide the blueprint for where you are taking your practice and how you will get there... but ultimately the plans are only as good as the execution. Establish processes such as the scorecard tracking and monthly progress reviews to monitor the implementation of your plans.

Business Plan Terminology is Confusing

There are no universally acceptable definitions to the terms Vision, Mission, Objectives, Strategies or Action Plans. How you use these terms depends entirely on what school you went to and what companies you have worked for. Many companies never successfully complete their business plans because they cannot agree on the basic terminology. We solved the problem!

We translated the five standard business plan elements into five simple and universal questions:

Vision: What are you building?

Mission: Why does this business exist?

Objectives: What results will you measure?

Strategies: How will you build this business?

Action Plans: What is the work to be done?

Writing a business plan for a department or program?

Modify the Mission and Strategy questions by replacing the word "business" with department or program:

Department Usage	**Program Usage**
Mission: Why does this department exist?	Mission: Why does this program exist?
Strategy: How will you build this department?	Strategy: How will you build this program?

Business Plans Can be Simple and Clean

The best way to understand The One Page Business Plan is to read one... One Page Business Plans can generally be read in about five minutes or less.

The HR Consulting Group

Sally McKenzie & Bob Wilson

Consolidated Plan

vision

Within the next 3 years grow The HR Consulting Group into a $1 million North Texas consulting and training company specializing in human resource training and consulting services for companies within a 50 mile radius of Dallas/Ft. Worth that have between 50 and 500 employees.

mission

Bring Preventative HR Programs to Growing Companies!

objectives

- Achieve FY sales of $350,000.
- Earn pre-tax profits of $75,000; after paying two partner salaries of $100,000.
- Consistently have partners bill out 6 days per month at $1,500 per day.
- Generate $40,000 from audits & assessments.
- Increase training program & product revenue from $7,500 a month to $10,000 by Aug. 30th.
- Increase ave. bi-weekly attendance at employer council meetings from 12 to 20 by May 15th.
- Produce six notable, publishable case studies this year.
- Take a minimum of 2 one-week vacations in the next twelve months.

strategies

- Become known for preventing catastrophic employee problems that destroy businesses.
- Attract clients with 50 to 500 employees, business owners who want preventive solutions.
- Promote initial trial through our monthly employer council meetings & low-cost guide books.
- Generate revenues thru preventive audits & assessments, training programs & consulting.
- Use technology/Internet for tele-classes, audits & assessments, & selling training guides.
- Strategically align our firm w/ local employment law attorneys, CPAs & business consultants.
- Continue to create books, guides, audiotapes, & assessment products from existing services.
- Build a business that is ultimately not dependent on my presence; which will make it sellable.

action plans

- Publish "Employer's Bill of Rights Handbook" by Feb. 28th.
- Complete Sexual Harassment, Family Leave & Diversity Guidebooks by April 20th.
- Launch "New Manager Training Series" May 1st; repeat program once in Q3 & Q4.
- Begin hosting monthly "Managers Problem Solving Roundtable" in July.
- Complete makeover of website & e-commerce systems by Sept. 30th.
- Introduce Smart System's web-employee appraisal process to our clients starting Nov. 1st.

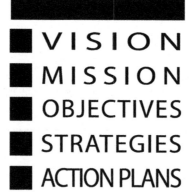

VISION
MISSION
OBJECTIVES
STRATEGIES
ACTION PLANS

Assessment

What's working? What's not?

"Too many people over plan and under execute.

Plan for what is critical... then execute the plan."

Intuitively you know the status of your consulting practice... but when is the last time you stopped and gave it a checkup? Took a real look under the hood?

The 10 Point Assessment on the next two pages is specifically designed for professional advisory practices like yours. These ten assessment areas should help you to quickly take the pulse of your company, which areas are strong, which aspects need attention... and those areas that you just have not gotten to yet.

Here are brief descriptions of the categories:

1.	New Client Acquisition	Outreach, introductions, referrals, on-boarding, engagement initiation
2.	Marketing	Branding, collateral, public relations, Internet
3.	Sales	Pipeline mgt, closing ratio, engagement size/value, add-on sales, repeat business
4.	Strategic Alliances	Referral resources, resource partners, product extension thru certifications, licensing, franchise
5.	Consulting Delivery	Deliverables, client satisfaction, scope mgt, quality, technology, stress level
6.	Public Speaking	Frequency, quality, audience ratings, impact
7.	Productization	Articles, books, software, audio/video products
8.	Professional Development	Research, seminars, advanced degrees
9.	Administrative Functions	Contracts, bookkeeping, taxes, technology
10.	Profitability/Cash Flow	Cash positive, adding to savings, taxes current

The left page is designed to help you quickly assess your total practice. The right page is designed to help you focus in at a more granular level. This entire exercise should take no more than about 15 minutes. Then move on. You can come back and reflect on it later as you are working on other aspects of your One Page Plan.

If you have multiple people in your practice, have everyone do the assessment and then compare and discuss the results.

What's Working in Your Consulting Practice?

Step 1: Rate each of these practice areas on a scale of 1 to 10; 1 = disaster 10 = brilliantly successful.

Step 2: Reflect on why you scored each element the way you did. Circle one or more of the reasons that influenced the rating. (FTI = Failure to Implement, ½♡ = half heartily executed plan, External = external forces, i.e. economy)

Practice Area	Significance Rating	Rating Scale
1. New Client Acquisition		1 2 3 4 5 6 7 8 9 10 FTI ½♡ People Process Time $$ External
2. Marketing		1 2 3 4 5 6 7 8 9 10 FTI ½♡ People Process Time $$ External
3. Sales		1 2 3 4 5 6 7 8 9 10 FTI ½♡ People Process Time $$ External
4. Strategic Alliances		1 2 3 4 5 6 7 8 9 10 FTI ½♡ People Process Time $$ External
5. Consulting Delivery		1 2 3 4 5 6 7 8 9 10 FTI ½♡ People Process Time $$ External
6. Public Speaking		1 2 3 4 5 6 7 8 9 10 FTI ½♡ People Process Time $$ External
7. Productization of Intellectual Property		1 2 3 4 5 6 7 8 9 10 FTI ½♡ People Process Time $$ External
8. Professional Development		1 2 3 4 5 6 7 8 9 10 FTI ½♡ People Process Time $$ External
9. Administrative Functions		1 2 3 4 5 6 7 8 9 10 FTI ½♡ People Process Time $$ External
10. Profitability/Cash Flow		1 2 3 4 5 6 7 8 9 10 FTI ½♡ People Process Time $$ External
Overall Assessment		**1 2 3 4 5 6 7 8 9 10**

Step 3: Make a check mark in the Significance Rating box for 3 to 4 elements you must dramatically improve in the next 6 to 12 months. It is highly doubtful you can make all of them 10s in the next year.

Key Projects... Specific Ideas for Improvement

In left column: Identify key projects or areas that influenced your assessment.
In right column: Quickly brainstorm actions that can be taken to improve execution/performance.

Key Projects	Action to Improve or Maintain

Example for New Client Acquisition:

New Client Campaign

More phone contact, less emphasis on collateral, more listening, offer better solutions

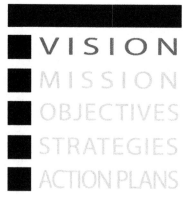

VISION

MISSION

OBJECTIVES

STRATEGIES

ACTION PLANS

The Vision Statement
What are you building?

"If you don't get the words right... you might build the wrong business!"

Everybody is building something... a company, an organization, or a department. Well-written Vision Statements answer the question: What is being built?... in three sentences or less!

Effective Vision Statements need not be long, but must clearly describe what you are building. A few key words will go a long way. Create a picture of what your company will look like in 1, 3 or even 5 years.

Vision Statements answer these questions:

- What type of company is this?
- What markets does it serve?
- What is the geographic scope?
- Who are the target customers?
- What are the key products and services?
- How big will the company be?
- What will revenues be?
- How many employees will there be?

Almost everyone has a Vision for their company, but some are better at articulating it. Many people struggle with capturing their Vision effectively in writing. At the One Page Business Plan Company we have learned that with a little prompting, most executives, even consultants can capture the essence of their Vision in just a few minutes.

Interview Exercise

Slightly overwhelmed? Want to make the process inclusive? Invite a trusted advisor to interview you using the questions below. Have them interview you in person or over the phone. Have them ask you the questions and record your responses. You might consider doing this interview process with more than one person.

1. Who's the perfect client?

Describe three characteristics of the ideal recipient of your service/product:

Describe three characteristics of clients you would be better off NOT SERVING:

2. What's the service or product?

Describe three characteristics of your service or product:

Describe three things your service or product WON'T DO:

3. What's the competitive environment?

Describe three characteristics of successful consulting practices you admire and WOULD like to emulate:

Describe three characteristics of consultants you WILL NOT emulate:

Getting the first draft onto paper is always the most difficult. It is infinitely easier to edit! The fill-in-the-blank-template below is geared to help you quickly create a first draft. Each blank in essence is a question; complete all the blanks, and you create a first draft... quickly and easily! Not able to fill in all of the blanks at this time? Don't worry... complete those that you can! Revisit the blanks later, you may need to do some research or enlist help from others.

Vision Statement

Within the next _____ years grow _____ into a $_____
(company name)   (est. annual sales)

_____   _____ company providing
(geographic scope)   (type of business)
(local/region/nat'l/int'l)

_____
(list 2-3 of your key products/services)

to _____.
(list 2-3 key clients/customers)

The following Vision Statement was created using the fill-in-the-blanks template and then edited. It is brief, but very clear.

> "Within the next 3 years grow CFO Consulting Services into a $250,000 San Francisco Bay Area financial management company specializing in strategic planning, budgeting, forecasting and other financial management best practices for companies that are large enough to have a Controller, but not large enough to have a full time Chief Financial Officer."

VISION
MISSION
OBJECTIVES
STRATEGIES
ACTION PLANS

Mission

Why does this consulting practice exist?

Mission Statements always answer the question, "Who will we serve and what will we do for them?"

Every company exists for a reason. Good Mission Statements describe why your product, service, department, project, program or business exists. Great Mission Statements are short and memorable. They communicate in just a few words (6 to 8 words are ideal) the company's focus and what is being provided to customers. They always answer the question, "Why will customers buy this product or service?"

Some of the best Mission Statements are an integral part of a company's branding strategy that compels customers to buy, but the same Mission Statements can and do direct and influence all significant management decisions.

Mission Statements answer these specific questions:

- Why does this business exist?
- What is our unique selling proposition?
- What are we committed to providing to our customers?
- What promise are we making to our clients?
- What wants, needs, desires, pain or problems do our products/services solve?

Crafting Your Mission Statement

Experiment with 6 to 8 key words (max. 12 words) that describe why your company exists from your customer's point of view. Capture your competitive marketing edge or unique selling proposition.

Why does this consulting practice exist?

1st Attempt:

We help _____ _____!
          (recipient of your services)   (goal or benefit of your services)

2nd Attempt:

3rd Attempt:

Examples of Mission Statements

The best Mission Statements are short and memorable! And eight words or less!

They may also evoke an emotional response through humor or the senses. Well-written Mission Statements attract customers and also drive behavior within an organization.

As you review these Company Mission Statements, ask yourself how well they answer the question, "Why does this company exist?"

ELA Consulting Group	We make companies smarter about their business!
Consulting CFOs	We are the small business financial navigators!
Entrepreneurial Authors	Every professional has a book in them... we help get it out!
Pratt Ranch Management	Healthy Land, Happy Families, Profitable Businesses... Ranching for Profit.
Nurseprenuer	We provide health care professionals training that prevents injuries and saves lives.
Beauty Resource	We're the Salon and Spa Business Experts!
ProAttitude	We end stress through a fundamental shift in attitude that restores the potential to be great!
Business Growth Strategies	We create break-through market plans!
Career Insights	We help people in career transition think "Outside the Cubicle".

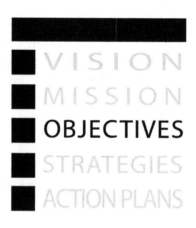

VISION
MISSION
OBJECTIVES
STRATEGIES
ACTION PLANS

Objectives

What will be measured?

Objectives are short statements that quantify the end results of any work effort. Good Objectives are easy to write and are instantly recognizable. They answer the question "What will we measure?"

Objectives clarify what you are trying to accomplish in specific, measurable terms. For an Objective to be effective, it needs to be a well-defined target with quantifiable elements. It is important to include different types of Objectives that cover the entire scope of your professional practice.

Well conceived Objectives:

- Provide a quantitative pulse of the business
- Focus resources towards specific results
- Define success in a measurable manner
- Give people/organizations specific targets
- Establish a framework for accountability and incentive pay
- Minimize subjectivity and emotionalism
- Measure the end results of work effort

Although there is no magical number of Objectives, a One Page Business Plan can accommodate nine. Consider two to three Objectives for sales or revenue, one for profitability, two or three for marketing, one or two that are process oriented.

Objectives Must be Graphable

The One Page methodology makes writing Objectives simple... All Objectives must be graphable!

Everyone learns early in their career that what you measure is what gets improved. If you are serious about growing a profitable consulting practice that is cash flow positive... chart your critical success factors. Have a chart for billable days or hours, total revenues, number of speaking engagements... whatever you know is critical for your success.

Charts are great... everybody can read charts. It's obvious when you are ahead of goal or not!

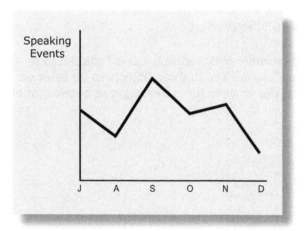

The key to setting meaningful Objectives is to identify goals that are:

- critical to your success and
- can be easily tracked
  (*Easily tracked = data is readily available & the specific target can be counted*)

Stated very simply, if you can not count it over time (easily)... it's not an Objective. On the Crafting Objectives exercise, we provide you with a number of frequently used goals in consulting firms... please note, all of them are graphable!

It's easy to craft meaningful Objectives when you use these 3 simple guidelines:

- Write only Objectives that can be graphed
- Include a numerical value in every Objective
- Assign a name & date to assure accountability

A Simple Formula for Writing Objectives...

> *Action To Be Taken*
> *+*
> *Something Countable*
> *+*
> *Target/Completion Date*

Here are some examples using this formula:

- Increase consulting revenues from $95,000 last year to $150,000 this year.

- Achieve profit before tax of $125,000.

- Sell 100 billable hours every month beginning June 1st.

- Add 10 new clients this year; 4 in 1st half, 2 in Q3 & 4 in Q4.

- Increase average consulting engagement from $15,000 to $25,000.

- Give at least 8 presentations in 1st half this year; 12 in 2nd half.

- Commit to writing 2 articles per quarter this year.

- Increase proprietary product sales from $30,000 to $70,000.

- Increase total hours per month of community service from 4 to 6 effective March 1st.

- Take a minimum of three weeks vacation this year.

- Increase number of free days per month from 1 to 3.

Crafting Your Objectives

Listed below are templates for Objectives that are fairly common for consulting firms. They are designed to help you quickly create a first draft. It is possible, but not likely all of these templates will work for your firm. If you do not see a template for an Objective that you need, create your own using the others as a model.

Sales	Achieve annual sales of $ _____.
Profit	Earn pre-tax profit this year of $ _____.
# of Clients	Increase number of active clients from _____ to _____.
Average Engagement	Increase average engagement from $_____ to $_____.
Project Sales	Sell _____ projects or engagements at $_____ for a total of $_____.
Billable Hours	Increase average monthly billable hours from _____ to _____.
Public Speaking	Give at least _____ presentations in 1st half; _____ in 2nd half.
Publishing	Commit to writing _____ articles per quarter this year. Total articles_____.
Product Sales	Increase _____ product sales from $_____ to $ _____.
Community Service	Increase (decrease) total hours of community service from _____ to _____.
Free Time	Commit to _____ weeks of vacation this year and _____ free days.

Remember, your One Page Plan can accommodate up to nine Objectives.

Sample Objectives...

Here are three sets of Objectives from three very different companies. In these examples there are 6 to 8 Objectives that describe "what these professional service firms will measure each month over the next 12 months to determine if they are on track." Some of these Objectives are rather traditional, others are a little unique. Hopefully they will get you to think creatively about your business... and what counts!

The Emergency IT Doctors

- Achieve annual sales of $500,000.
- Earn pre-tax profit of $60,000 after paying expenses and 3 principal salaries of $100,000.
- Increase number of active clients from 100 to 150 by June 30th.
- Reduce average client downtime from 6 hours to 4 hours.
- Reduce crisis response time from 2 hours to 1 hour.
- Increase percent of clients on remote technical service support program from 38% to 65%.
- Secure 150 PC audits in first six months of year to assure 33% conversion ratio.
- Reduce average OT from 26% to 10% by supplementing permanent staff w/ qualified temps.

Wealth Builders

- Increase assets under management from $15 to $25 million.
- Increase income after business expenses from $150,000 to $220,000 this year.
- Increase ROA from .85% to 1.0%
- Increase average acct. from $250,000 to $600,000 in three years; $350,000 by Dec. 31st.
- Increase number of active accounts from 60 to 72 by year end.
- Volunteer 10 hours a month with the American Red Cross.
- Take a total of 30 days of vacation and free days this year.

Leaders by Design

- Achieve annual consulting revenues of $175,000.
- Earn pre-tax profit of $105,000.
- Increase number of active clients from 4 to 6 by July 1st.
- Speak at least once a month in 1st half of year, 10 times in 2nd half; total speaking gigs 16.
- Produce one Leadership by Design executive retreat per quarter; yielding $15,000 each.
- Create & publish one 600 to 800 word article per month; be positioned to write book this year.
- Reduce personal time on administrivia to less than 6 hours per week.
- Decrease my weight from 210 to 180 pounds by year end.

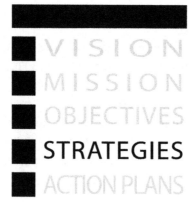

VISION
MISSION
OBJECTIVES
STRATEGIES
ACTION PLANS

Strategies

How will this business be built?

*"Strategies
define what
will make your
consulting
practice
successful
over time!"*

Success is rarely an accident. It is usually the result of executing a carefully crafted set of strategies. Strategies provide a blueprint or road map for building and managing the company. They also provide a comprehensive overview of the company's business model and frequently say as much about what the company will not do, as what it will do.

Strategies set the direction, philosophy, values, and methodology for building and managing your company. They establish guidelines and boundaries for evaluating business decisions. Following a predefined set of strategies is critical to keeping a business on track.

One way of understanding strategies is to think of them as industry practices. Every industry has its leaders, its followers and its rebels, and each has an approach for capturing market share. Pay attention to the successful businesses in your industry and you can learn important lessons. You can also learn a lot from the failures in your industry.

Strategies are not secret. In fact they are common knowledge and openly shared in every industry. Pick up any industry's publication and you will know precisely what the industry's leaders have to say about the opportunities and how to capitalize on them. These leaders will also share their current problems and their solutions. This is critical information for building and managing your business. Capture the best thinking/best practices from your industry along with the strategies that make your company distinct and you will have a powerful set of strategies that drive your company forward!

In summary, Strategies are broad statements, covering multiple years that:

- Set the direction, philosophy, values
- Define the business model
- Establish guidelines for evaluating important decisions
- Set limits on what a company will do or will not do

Components of a Successful Practice

There are many moving parts to a successful consulting practice. There are a lot of decisions to be made. Many of the decisions are personal preference.

Keep in mind that nobody gets all the parts and pieces in place before they start... it takes time; probably three to five years. Review this list; use it as a catalyst to think about what will actually be necessary to make your consulting practice successful over time. As you are crafting your Strategies on page 40, refer back to this page.

- ☐ Personal Expertise
- ☐ Business Success
- ☐ Technical Knowledge
- ☐ Reputation
- ☐ Referral Sources
- ☐ Partners or Going Solo
- ☐ Strategic Alliances
- ☐ Company Image
- ☐ Market Presence
- ☐ Uniqueness of Offering
- ☐ Product Name
- ☐ Branding
- ☐ Ideal Customers
- ☐ No. of Clients

- ☐ Value Proposition
- ☐ Price Point: Hi, Mid, Low
- ☐ Importance of Quality
- ☐ Availability & Access
- ☐ Productizing Your Services
- ☐ Publishing: Self or Trade
- ☐ Speaking: Free or Paid
- ☐ Hi or Low Tech Products
- ☐ Build or Buy Products
- ☐ Licensing & Franchising
- ☐ Sell Only Your Services
- ☐ Sell Other People's Time
- ☐ Sell Other People's Skills
- ☐ Shared Support Services

- ☐ Trademarks/Patents
- ☐ Geographical Area Served
- ☐ Customer Service
- ☐ Board of Advisors
- ☐ Use of Technology
- ☐ Employees
- ☐ Home Office or Downtown
- ☐ Part or Full Time
- ☐ Self-funding
- ☐ Loans or Capital
- ☐ Amount of Travel
- ☐ Family Support
- ☐ Peace of Mind
- ☐ Amount of Free Time

Deciding Which Strategies Are Appropriate for Your Business

Finding appropriate strategies for your business is not difficult. As you can see from the list above... there are many choices.

Much information is readily available to you for free or at minimal cost. There are probably multiple professional trade associations that serve your niche. Go online and explore. Ask other consultants in your niche where to go to research the latest trends in your industry.

The key question is: which strategies will you select... and at what time in the life cycle of your company? You cannot execute all of your strategies at the same time.

In the early stages of your practice, it is critical that you employ strategies that leverage your expertise, career successes, and your extensive network. Yes, your network is extensive; you may need to rediscover it.

In the early stages pro bono work can be invaluable to help people understand that you are now available in a new capacity.

The most important strategy might be for you to become know as a source of referrals. Want referrals? Give them freely, regularly!

Research Exercise

Review the last three issues of your industry's trade, professional or association journals and answer the questions below.

What and where are the opportunities?	How can you capitalize on them?

What threats exist?	How can you minimize the threats and/or turn them into opportunities?

Examples of Issues Affecting Consulting & Professional Service Firms

- Shortage of qualified people
- Client companies demanding more, but may have smaller budgets.
- Consultants are getting older, not willing to work as long as they used to.
- Experienced consultants less willing to have all of their eggs tied up with one or two clients.

- Hourly & daily rate resistance
- Travel has become a major hassle. Consultants less willing to jump on an airplane.
- Use of executive/professional coaches becoming accepted.

A Simple Formula for Writing Strategies...

> *Define business growth*
> *or*
> *improvement process*
> *+*
> *How it will be achieved*

Here are some examples using this formula:

Positioning	Become nationally known for solving leadership issues in hospitals.
Perfect Client	Attract/solicit clients that need to master Internet marketing.
Opportunities	Focus on trend to hire baby boomers as supplemental workforce.
Products/ Services	Core services are market research, focus groups & analytical consumer studies.
Initial Trial	Promote initial trial w/ public speaking, free assessments & limited scope projects.
Revenue Model	Generate revenues by sale of services, product sales, public speaking.
Pricing	Price our services at slight premium to market, justified by national recognition.
Consulting Delivery	Primary consulting will be done by me; supplement w/core team of trusted experts.
Technology/ Internet	Use technology/Internet for building awareness/credibility, productization of services.
Strategic Alliances	Use strategic alliances to co-brand, co-market, co-sell & productization.
Productization	Create books, audio tapes & software based on the Always Get the Sale™ process.
Administration	Minimize personal time on admin functions; use part time asst.; invest in software.

The One Page Practice Development Plan

We call this exercise, Bend the Curve.

Step 1: Draft a Revenue Objective for your consulting practice for the next 1, 3 or 5 years.
Step 2: Brainstorm up to four Strategies that are necessary to achieve the Objective in Step 1.
Step 3: Identify 2 to 4 key Action Plans per Strategy. Action Plans are typically Projects or Programs.

Increase _____ from _____ to _____ by _____.

(Example: Increase client count from 100 to 200 by 12/31)

Strategy

Strategy

Strategy

Strategy

Action Plans

_____   _____   _____   _____

_____   _____   _____   _____

_____   _____   _____   _____

Listed below is a set of Strategy templates that are common for consulting firms. The templates are designed to help you quickly create a first draft. It is unlikely your firm will need all of these Strategies, but this set of templates should help you focus on how you will build your consulting practice... and what will make it successful over time.

Positioning	Become nationally known for solving _____ & _____ problems.
Perfect Client	Attract/solicit clients that need _____, _____ & _____.
Opportunities	Focus on _____, _____ & _____ trends/opportunities.
Products/Services	Core products/services are _____, _____ & _____.
Revenue Model	Generate revenues by _____, _____ & _____.
Pricing	Our pricing strategy is _____, _____ & _____.
Initial Trial	Promote initial trial by _____, _____ & _____.
Consulting Delivery	Consulting will be delivered by _____, _____ & _____.
Technology/Internet	Use technology/Internet for _____, _____ & _____.
Strategic Alliances	Use strategic alliances to _____, _____ & _____.
Productization	Create _____, _____ & _____ products from _____ services.

Remember, your One Page Plan can accommodate up to nine Strategies.

Sample Strategies...

Here are three sets of strategies, from three very different companies. In these examples there are 6 to 8 strategies that describe the "essence of what will make these companies successful over time." These strategies describe business models, best practices, culture and personal preferences. All were initially created with the fill-in-the-blank templates and then edited. Note that each strategy fits on a single line.

The HR Consulting Group

- Become known for preventing catastrophic employee problems that destroy businesses.
- Attract clients with 50 to 500 employees, business owners who want preventive solutions.
- Promote initial trial through monthly employer council meetings & low-cost guide books.
- Generate revenues thru preventive audits & assessments, training programs & consulting.
- Use technology/Internet for tele-classes, audits & assessments & selling training guides.
- Strategically align our firm w/ local employment law attorneys, CPAs & business consultants.
- Continue to create books, guides, audiotapes & assessment products from existing services.
- Build a business that is ultimately not dependent on my presence; making it sellable.

Consulting CFOs

- Focus on companies w/ sales of $3 to $30 million not large enough to have a FT CFO.
- Core advisory services: planning, budgeting, forecasting, cash mgt, financing, risk mgmt.
- Promote initial trial by public speaking, low-cost financial capabilities assessment & seminars.
- Generate revenues thru consulting, CFO & Controller searches, seminars & product commissions.
- Price offerings to yield high margins by bundling services w/ high-value web tools/software.
- Consulting delivered by senior partners, analysis by senior accountants; selectively outsource.
- Use web-based budgeting, planning software apps. that minimize need for client site visits.
- Get referrals by generously giving tax work to CPAs & legal issues to attorneys.

Main Street Business Strategy Group

- Become nat'ly known for renovating 1960s strip malls into vibrant, profitable retail destinations.
- Focus on nat'l trend to revitalize the downtown retail experience.
- Partner w/ real estate developers, boutique & nat'l brand retailers, city redevelopment agencies.
- Primarily generate revenues thru consulting services: research, design, plans and advocacy.
- Use technology/Internet to facilitate research, focus groups, community involvement & advocacy.
- Build nat'l brand & corporate identity by creatively showcasing success stories on national media.

Sage Advice from Successful Consultants...

Consultants talk too much... especially during the sales process. Frequently after listening to a prospect for just a few minutes, they think they have more than enough information to propose one or more solutions. I suggest at the point a consultant thinks they know enough to propose a solution... they take a deep breath, and ask another question! And a few minutes later, when once again they think they have enough information to propose a solution... STOP, take another deep breath... and ask another question. After a consultant has repeated this process three, four or five times... they might know enough to propose a solution. But not necessarily!

Harvey Meier, Harvey A. Meier Co., Inc., Spokane, Washington

Many consultants are uncomfortable discussing pricing and the terms of their consulting engagement face to face. We all too often allow our fear and assumptions sabotage us. I suggest when it's time to talk price, a consultant should take a deep breath, maybe two -- look 'em in the eye, and state their price... without apology.

Toni Nell, Springboard Consulting, Santa Cruz, California

Consultants typically think the sales process is over once they have the CEO's buy-in. In fact, the sale to the CEO, business owner or executive is just the first sale. Regardless of the nature of the consulting engagement, the consultant will almost always have to resell the project to each and every person involved with the project to assure that they will fully participate. The key to successful projects is to have all of the participants understand how their involvement in the project will personally benefit them.

Chuck Fry, Fry Consulting Group, Alameda, California

Most consultants' approach to networking is horrible! They go from one leads group or professional organization to another hoping, sometimes pressuring people into giving them introductions and referrals. And then they wonder why they never get referrals. My suggestion is simple: Get involved with the professional and business groups that make sense for your company. Show up regularly and do everything you can possibly do to help the people in that organization grow their business. Your generosity will come back to you, and your business will grow too! And don't forget: the easiest way to get referrals is to give them.

Jeff Rubin, The Newsletter Guy, Pinole, California

Sometimes, in an earnest quest to offer a solution to our client's need we inadvertently try to close a sale prematurely. What I notice and feel is an instant awkwardness. Other times I may begin to experience that sinking feeling we call rejection. What I have come to learn in either case is my focus has shifted from the client... to me! I am beginning to feel sorry or bad about a pending loss of something I do not even own. That moment of awkwardness is the place where the "business transaction" has overtaken "relationship building". The solution is actually very easy: ask another question! Questions, when from real curiosity, will always shift the focus from you back to the client... where it should be!

Brenda Chaddock, Limitless Leadership, Vancouver, British Columbia

and Corporate Buyers of Consulting Services

An internal consultant with a Fortune 500 company who has purchased millions of dollars of training and consulting over the last 25+ years shared these observations about consultants and their behavior during the bidding and proposal stage of a multi-million dollar consulting engagement.

1. First consultants eliminated were ME CENTERED... they dominated the conversation, told all about their processes, products, past clients. It was all about them. They asked few questions.

2. Second set of consultants eliminated were CONTENT or FACT CENTERED... they knew everything about everything. They quoted all of the latest management books, they were able to quote facts from all of the top surveys and analyses. They had a quote, a fact and the references to back up everything they said. They were undoubtedly very knowledgeable... but without a doubt, they were not going to work with this client.

3. Third set of consulting firms eliminated were PRODUCT CENTERED... these firms offered their product solutions long before they understood the underlying problems. These firms were outstanding at demo-ing their products and espousing the features of the products... .but nobody cared. These firms took no time to understand the real underlying issues.

4. The final two firms were CLIENT ORIENTED... they took time to fully interview the prospective client and understand the underlying issues. They asked tons of questions... finally the interviewing team asked the consultants if they thought they had a solution to the problem. I believe they then asked another question (just joking).

Take time to get to know your prospects... and, "just about the time you think you are ready to offer a solution, ask another question!"

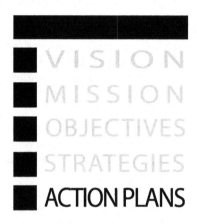

VISION
MISSION
OBJECTIVES
STRATEGIES
ACTION PLANS

Action Plans

Defining the Work to be Done

"Business building projects always compete with marketing and revenue production.

Commit to 1 to 2 major projects per year! They will serve you well!"

Action Plans define the actual work to be done... the specific actions the business must take to implement Strategies and to achieve the Objectives.

For your consulting practice, Action Plans will be major business-building or infrastructure projects. They will undoubtedly focus on the execution of your Marketing, Technology and Productization projects. These projects may require significant capital and expense budgets; for sure they will consume your valuable time, and may take multiple months to complete.

In well-written One Page Business Plans, Action Plans are NEVER "job description tasks".

Ideally, each Action Plan statement relates to an Objective or a Strategy... but it is not necessary to write an Action Plan for every Objective or Strategy in your One Page Business Plan. You will not have enough space... and more importantly you will not have enough time or money to execute all of the projects you can dream up. Your One Page Plan will accommodate up to nine major plans. We suggest you craft no more than two plans per quarter. For small consulting companies... one major project, like writing a book... may be all that is reasonable to accomplish in one year.

Remember: Your One Page Business Plan is designed to capture the most important elements of your plan... not all of the elements. If you find that nine Action Plans are not enough, it's possible you may need to write a separate One Page Plan for one or more of the larger projects... or more likely, you have defined too many projects for this year.

"Work" may be defined three ways:

- Major business-building projects
- Significant infrastructure projects
- Programs/Projects that bend the curves and/or trend lines

A Simple Formula for Writing Action Plans...

Description of Work + Completion Date

Here are some examples using the formula:

- Complete the "Selling Made Easy" book by March 31st,; 1st print run by May 31st.
- Launch 2nd quarter Executive Briefing Series w/ "Stress-Free Management" on April 15th.
- Complete re-design of website with e-commerce capabilities by July 31st.
- Build prototype web application to simplify employee appraisal by Oct. 31st.
- Hire part-time administrative assistant by February 28th; Bookkeeper by April 30th.

Work "Bends" the Curve... Project Prioritization

In the Strategy section we used the "Bend the Curve" visual to identify the major opportunities that have the potential to significantly grow your business over the next 3 to 5 years. We can again use this visual model to help identify and prioritize the major projects and programs you and your team are going to focus on in the next twelve months.

When you have agreed on the projects that will bend the curve, assign completion dates and responsibility... then craft the Action Plans. Each of these projects is a potential candidate for your One Page Business Plan! Also be sure to calculate the expense and capital budgets for these projects and get them into your One Page Budget Worksheet, which is included in the Consultant's eToolkit.

Bend the Curve
Projects that Produce Results

Identify 2 to 4 projects or programs you are going to implement this year that have the greatest potential for Bending the Curve(s) in your consulting practice. You might have a Bend the Curve worksheet for Sales, Profitability, Market Awareness and Productivity! Or you might just have one for the entire company. Remember: keep it simple. If a little is good, more does not necessarily make it better.

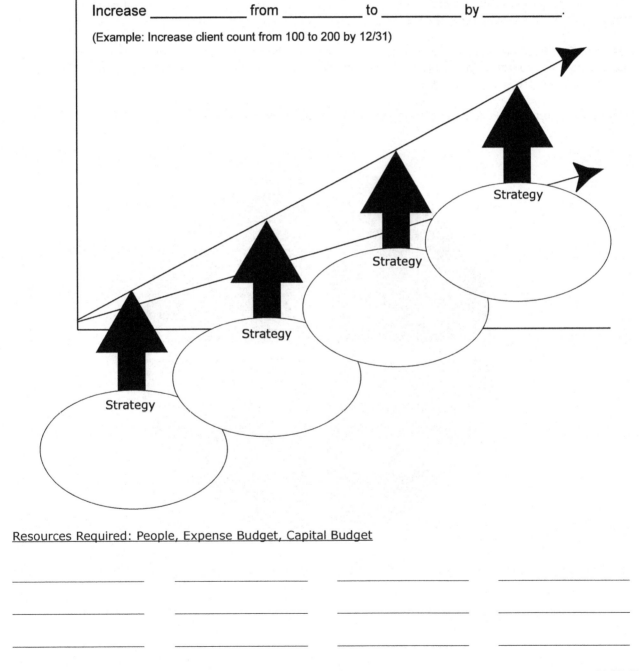

Increase _____ from _____ to _____ by _____.

(Example: Increase client count from 100 to 200 by 12/31)

Strategy

Strategy

Strategy

Strategy

Resources Required: People, Expense Budget, Capital Budget

_____   _____   _____   _____

_____   _____   _____   _____

_____   _____   _____   _____

The One Page Planning Wheel

The One Page Planning Wheel is another visual tool that helps entrepreneurs, business owners and executives visualize key projects over the entire year.

Most people have little problem identifying critical tasks and near-term projects that need to be completed in the next six days... or six weeks. But the identification, prioritization and calendaring of significant projects and programs in the second half of the year... or beyond, can be difficult when the focus is so often on short term results.

Use The One Page Planning Wheel as a tool to brainstorm the key projects in your company, division, department or program. In the brainstorming phase, identify all major projects, then refine the list down to two or three projects per quarter.

Remember, your One Page Business Plan can accommodate up to nine Action Plans.

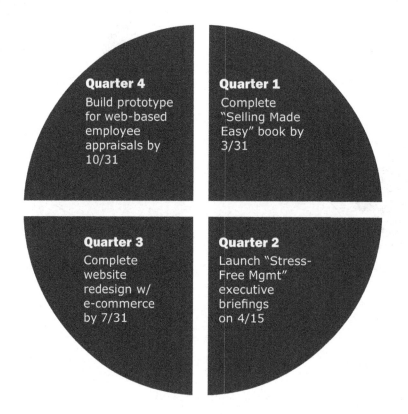

Quarter 4
Build prototype for web-based employee appraisals by 10/31

Quarter 1
Complete "Selling Made Easy" book by 3/31

Quarter 3
Complete website redesign w/ e-commerce by 7/31

Quarter 2
Launch "Stress-Free Mgmt" executive briefings on 4/15

Crafting Your Action Plans

There are four quarters in a year. List one or two major business-building projects that must be accomplished in each of the next four quarters in order to implement your strategies and achieve your overall goals. When complete, type your Action Plans into The One Page Business Plan template that is in the Consultant's eToolkit.

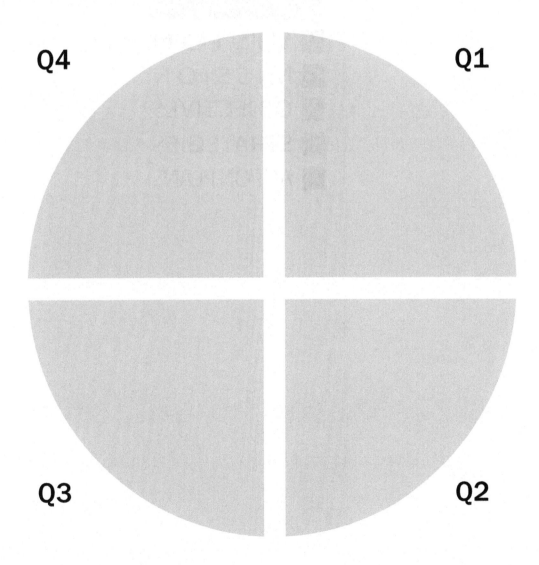

Remember: Time exists so that you do not have to do everything at once.

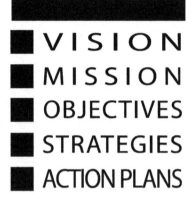

VISION
MISSION
OBJECTIVES
STRATEGIES
ACTION PLANS

Assembling and Polishing the Plan

"Congratulations! Your Plan is Now in Writing... What's Next?"

Assemble Your Plan onto One Page!

Select one of The One Page Business Plan templates from the Consultant's eToolkit and type in each of the five elements of the plan you created using the various exercises. See last page for eToolkit link.

Step Back and Review Your Plan

How does it look to you? If you are like most people, some parts of your plan will be complete, while other parts will still need editing and additional detail. Don't rush the process! Make the obvious changes now, but allow some time to reflect on your plan.

Carry the plan with you; it's only one page! As new ideas and insights appear, capture them on paper. Review the Polishing and Edit suggestions on the next page. Most people find it takes about three drafts to get their plans in solid shape... don't cut the process short. Too much depends on it.

Review Your Plan with Others

You have a plan... now review it with your partners, team, and/or trusted advisors. Have them ask you clarifying questions. Take good notes on the feedback; you might consider recording the feedback sessions. Update your plan with the feedback you decide is appropriate.

Have Partners? Employees? Have them Create their One Page Business Plan

Executives, managers, teams and partners are expensive! After you have reviewed your plan with your team, and they have had a chance to ask clarifying questions, give them 3 to 7 business days to create their One Page Business Plan. Encourage them to work together; the plans will be more cohesive as a result.

Balance and Align the Plans

Balancing the plans is a process that ensures all of the functions within your company will be working together, on the right projects and programs, in the proper sequence, at the right time... and not at cross purposes.

When your organization's plans are balanced and aligned... you can have everyone, literally, working on the same page!

Editing and Polishing the Plan

Here is a list of ideas and tips to polish your plan:

Overall Review

- Does your Vision Statement describe what you are building?
- Will your Mission Statement attract new clients? Drive employee behavior? Is it memorable?
- Are your Objectives measurable, dated and graphable?
- Do your Strategies describe what will make your business successful over time?
- Are your Action Plans significant business-building projects? Will they achieve your Objectives?

Order and Abbreviation

- Edit Objectives, Strategies, and Action Plan statements to one line.
- Eliminate all unnecessary words and phrases.
- Abbreviate words when necessary.
- Use symbols like "&" in lieu of "and" to save space.
- Use "k" or "m" for thousands and "M" for millions.
- Communicate priority of Objectives, Strategies, and Action Plans by placing them in the proper order.

Creative Considerations

- Use bullets to make key points stand out.
- Highlight key phrases in italics.

Strengthening Exercises

- Edit Vision, Mission and Strategy until they are enduring statements that "resonate!"
- Drop low-priority items. Remember, "less can produce more."
- Refine Objectives and Action Plans to be specific, measurable, and define accountability.

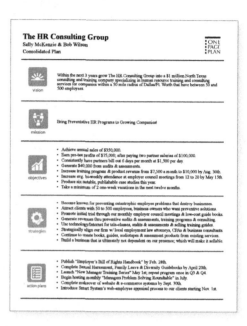

Involve Others

- Few people can write a solid plan by themselves; ask others for feedback.
- Ask your reviewers:
    - Is this plan really strategic? Too optimistic? Too pessimistic?
    - Does it include all of the critical initiatives you have been talking about?
    - Is it too risky? Too safe?
    - Does it reflect your best thinking?
    - What have I overlooked? What do you see that I missed?
- Listen to the feedback, take notes, and ask clarifying questions.
- Revise and update plan for feedback.
- Ask for another round of feedback.
- Most people find it takes at least three drafts to have a solid plan.
- Repeat until you and your reviewers agree it is solid.

Resources, Timelines and Budgets

Having a plan is critical to your success. Here are a few thoughts on other important processes that will help assure your success.

Define the Required Resources

Every project, program and initiative in your plan will need resources... or it will not happen. For each project identify the people, expense, capital budgets and any other resources required to fully execute the plan. The process of identifying the resources may cause you to realize you may not have the capability or capacity of implementing the plan you just wrote. If that is the case, go back and revise the plan.

Project Timelines

Re-review your project start and completion dates. Are they realistic? One of the major problems with all planning processes is the tendency to think we can do more than we actually can. When we complete a major project or initiative... we feel smart! When we have a list of projects that we have not started or are half done... we feel defeated. Take another hard look at your projects for this next year... would you be extraordinarily pleased if you completed just one or two of them? If so, adjust your plan.

Alignment with Partners & Team

If you have partners or a team, it is not unusual to find during the alignment process that the business units within your company contributing to projects and programs will not have consistent and appropriate start and completion times. For each major project or program, create an overall timeline to assure all of the sub-tasks are in alignment with the overall milestones. If project dates get changed... be sure to update the plans accordingly.

Create a Budget

Almost every activity in a business has a stream of revenue or expenses associated with it. Use your One Page Business Plan(s) to help identify all of the sources of revenue, expense and capital. If you need help in budgeting, get it. This is an important part of your success. Included in the Consultant's eToolkit is a simple One Page Budget Worksheet that should be helpful. See link at the back of the book

Recommendation: If a business unit is big enough for a One Page Business Plan, it should have a separate budget.

Implementation... Tracking & Measuring the Plan

Implement Your Plan

Many plans fail because they never get implemented! When great ideas sit on the shelf... nothing happens. Put your plan to work. You can bet your competitors are working on theirs!

Monitor & Measure

There are a number of resources in the eToolkit that comes with this book, (find the download link on the last page in this book), but that's only a start in terms of measuring progress towards your goals. Even more powerful is our cloud-based One Page Planning and Performance System available through our network of licensed affiliates. It will help you create a simple and easy to use framework for monitoring and measuring progress towards your goals. See a short four minute demonstration video at www.onepagebusinessplan.com/solutions/tour-our-system

Monthly Business Review

Recent surveys indicate only 1 in 5 businesses have a regularly scheduled monthly business review meeting to monitor both the implementation and execution of their plans.

The monthly business review is a fabulous opportunity to learn what really happens in your business each month. Do a quick review of each of the major projects... are they on track? If not, address the issues and define solutions to get them back on track. One way to accomplish this is with our One Page Planning and Performance System shown here. To learn more go to www.onepagebusinessplan.com

Filling in the Gaps

The process of writing a business plan, in some ways, is like writing a term paper on your business. You capture in writing what you know, conduct research to fill in the gaps, interview knowledgeable people, draft your document, ask for feedback, and then complete the final editing.

Your knowledge of your business is significant. Capture your initial thoughts in the first draft, and then begin the process of reflecting on your plan... and involving others. Keep in mind, the process of planning is one of continual reflection and refinement... and in many ways this is more important than the final document.

Most people have more resources instantly available to them than they realize. These resources are very knowledgeable... and frequently free! They know you, your business, the industry, may share the same clients and may buy from the same vendors.

Resources readily available to you include your team, peer managers, senior executives, Board of Directors, Board of Advisors, vendors, bankers, attorneys, CPAs, and other consultants.

Other significant resources are the national trade associations. They exist to gather and disseminate information about your industry. They follow all of the trends, innovations, opportunities, regulations, etc. Check out their websites, better yet pick up the phone and talk with one of the executives. Get to know the regular contributors.

One of the benefits of The One Page Business Plan is that it can be read in less than five minutes. Share your plan with your resources. Invite their insights and feedback. Your plan will be stronger!

"Your plan is not finished until it represents your best thinking!"

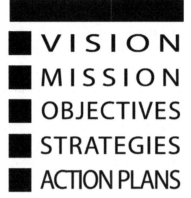

VISION
MISSION
OBJECTIVES
STRATEGIES
ACTION PLANS

Sample Plans...

"The One Page Plan methodology is extremely flexible.

Since 1994, over 500,000 companies have created One Page Plans!"

For some, the easiest way to learn how to write a plan is to take a look at how others have written their plans. In this section we have provided four consulting company plans for your review and many more plans that show the breadth and flexibility of The One Page Business Plan methodology.

There are sample plans for:

- Consulting firms
  - Human Resources
  - Automation Services
  - Management Services
  - Seminar company

- Large corporation
  - Consolidated Plan
  - Sales Division
  - Staff function (2)

- Mfg. & Distribution Company
- Government Agency
- Non-Profits
- Church
- Associations
- and Others

As you review these plans, you will note that they all follow the One Page Methodology fairly closely... but not necessarily... precisely. That's OK! Each of these plans is a real plan, written by an executive, business owner or entrepreneur... so their personal style comes through!

Note: Sample plans have these consistent characteristics

- Vision Statements paint a graphical picture of what is being built.
- Mission Statements are short, most are 8 words or less.
- Objectives are always graphable!
- Strategies describe how the non-profit, department, project or program will be built.
- Action Plans describe the work to be done... all have completion dates.

The HR Consulting Group

Sally McKenzie & Bob Wilson

Consolidated Plan

vision

Within the next 3 years grow The HR Consulting Group into a $1 million North Texas consulting and training company specializing in human resource training and consulting services for companies within a 50 mile radius of Dallas/Ft. Worth that have between 50 and 500 employees.

mission

Bring Preventative HR Programs to Growing Companies!

objectives

- Achieve FY sales of $350,000.
- Earn pre-tax profits of $75,000; after paying two partner salaries of $100,000.
- Consistently have partners bill out 6 days per month at $1,500 per day.
- Generate $40,000 from audits & assessments.
- Increase training program & product revenue from $7,500 a month to $10,000 by Aug. 30th.
- Increase ave. bi-weekly attendance at employer council meetings from 12 to 20 by May 15th.
- Produce six notable, publishable case studies this year.
- Take a minimum of 2 one-week vacations in the next twelve months.

strategies

- Become known for preventing catastrophic employee problems that destroy businesses.
- Attract clients with 50 to 500 employees, business owners who want preventive solutions.
- Promote initial trial through our monthly employer council meetings & low-cost guide books.
- Generate revenues thru preventive audits & assessments, training programs & consulting.
- Use technology/Internet for tele-classes, audits & assessments, & selling training guides.
- Strategically align our firm w/ local employment law attorneys, CPAs & business consultants.
- Continue to create books, guides, audiotapes, & assessment products from existing services.
- Build a business that is ultimately not dependent on my presence; which will make it sellable.

action plans

- Publish "Employer's Bill of Rights Handbook" by Feb. 28th.
- Complete Sexual Harassment, Family Leave & Diversity Guidebooks by April 20th.
- Launch "New Manager Training Series" May 1st; repeat program once in Q3 & Q4.
- Begin hosting monthly "Managers Problem Solving Roundtable" in July.
- Complete makeover of website & e-commerce systems by Sept. 30th.
- Introduce Smart System's web-employee appraisal process to our clients starting Nov. 1st.

Future Best Practices, Inc.

James McIntire, President

Business Plan

---

vision

Within five years, become nationally known author, publisher, speaker and consultant serving entrepreneurs and independent business owners. Consult primarily in greater Boston metro area; approximately 30% of my time. Create products (books, MP3s, CDs) for the entrepreneurial market 25% of my time. Speak extensively regionally, building to national recognition. This year, total revenues will be $175,000 or more.

---

mission

We help business owners build strong companies with best practices!

---

objectives

- Generate total revenues of $175,000 this year.
- Achieve profit before tax of $90,000 this year.
- Increase active consulting client base from 20 to 30; increase consulting fees to $90k.
- Secure 12 paid speaking engagements by 10/31 at average fee of $2,500.
- Sell 1,000 books by 12/31.
- Train 10 registered/certified E-Mgmt practitioners by 12/31.
- Sell 500 E-Mgmt. MP3s yielding $5,000 by 12/31.
- Sell 500 copies of my "No Accident" book by 12/31.

---

strategies

- Collaborate to complete; can't do this by myself... Always keep it simple!
- Use personal contacts to create opportunities to speak, get reviews, articles published.
- Self publish to start, prove marketability, seek national publisher.
- Create products & programs for others to sell that serve the entrepreneurial market.
- Seek endorsement/approval/intros; Quotes from noted authors, CEOs, SBA.
- Build national brand & corporate identity.
- Exit strategy; sell to major publisher or business training company in 5-7 years.

---

action plans

- Complete E-Mgmt book. by April 25th; print 6,000 copies by May 31st.
- Publish article in Inc. Magazine in 4th quarter.
- Develop publicity & marketing plans by 3/31.
- Develop E-Mgmt Certification program by 7/31.
- Contract w/Audio Design Productions for audio tape production by 7/15.
- Submit articles to Inc., Entrepreneur, Home Base Business for December publication.
- Complete mailing to 250 trade associations by 8/15 for speaking engagements.

ZXM Automation Consulting, Inc.

Allen Marcus, President

Consolidated Plan

vision

Within the next five years build ZXM Automation into the premier west coast industrial process automation consulting company specializing in integration solutions. ZXM Automation revenues will grow from $10 million last year to $20 million in five years by expanding its role from a manufacturing representative company to a complete engineering field service and process solutions company.

mission

Helping you control your marketing, sales, service and distribution channels!

objectives

- Grow business 20% & achieve total sales revenues of $12 million this year.
- Achieve profit before tax of $1 million.
- Land at least 5 significant system projects at a minimum of $250k each this year.
- Increase gross margin from 17% to 20%.
- Increase sales per employee from $320,000 to $375,000.
- Increase Engineering Services billable utilization from 50% to 70%.

strategies

- Sell total solutions not parts.
- Significantly increase valued added engineering & integration service capabilities.
- Expand geographically into So. Calif., Oregon/Washington, Nevada, Arizona, Alaska.
- Aggressively target niche markets in each geographic market.
- Expand thru selective acquisitions and/or strategic partnerships.
- Continually develop the discipline of profitability for ZXM & our clients.
- Attract/retain key employees by maximizing their creative, technical & business talents.
- Share growth & prosperity w/ employees through incentive & equity participation

action plans

- Critical Marketing Program: Visit all 25 base system clients in 2nd Q.
- Hire System Eng. by 4/30 and Sales Mgr. by 6/30.
- Implement Client Awareness & F2K Support Programs in 3rd Q.
- Complete UC Berkeley, Lipton, SAI projects successfully by 9/30.
- Implement F2K Demo website in 4th Q.
- Install new NT server by 3/31 & Unix server in 2nd Q.
- Implement Sales Automation Program and complete conference room demo in 3rd Q.
- Complete business practices, procedures & policy manual by 12/31.

Jordan Business Seminars

Tom Jordan, Owner

Business Plan Summary

vision

Within the next year, build a highly efficient marketing program to catapult our web graphics seminar business to $500,000 annual revenues.

mission

Help graphic artists migrate their businesses to the web!

objectives

- Sell 2000 Seminar seats nationally in the next 12 months yielding $408,000 in revenue.
- Sell an average of $46 per attendee books and tapes at each seminar; $92,000 in revenue.
- Earn a pre-tax profit of 25% or $125,000.
- Increase gross margin to 72% on seminar seats.
- Maintain COGS on books and tapes at 66%.

strategies

- Direct mail to purchasers of Adobe Products.
- Stress the business opportunity rather than the fact they will be learning software.
- Offer book and tape set bundles to increase average purchase.
- Increase the amount of on-site sales people to increase seminar sales.
- End quantity discounts on multiple sign-ups from single company.
- Utilize temp agencies in each seminar city to supply additional sales help.

action plans

- Redesign seminar mailer to stress business opportunity by January 15th.
- Design promotional piece to highlight better margin book and tape bundles by April 1st.
- Launch email newsletter to promote seminars by June 30th.
- Hire writer by March 3rd to edit new online newsletter.

Z-TEC, Inc. – Consolidated Plan

Jerome Johnson, CEO

FY Plan

vision

Within the next three years build Z-TEC, Inc. into a $2 billion global provider of integrated workflow management solutions for Fortune 1000 companies, major municipalities and significant governmental agencies at the country, state, regional and federal level. Z-TEC, Inc. will be headquartered in San Francisco with offices in New York, Dallas, London, Singapore and Rio de Janeiro.

mission

Building Industrial Strength Business Systems!

objectives

- FY Revenue of at least $900 Million.
- FY Profit before Interest & Taxes of $85 Million.
- Complete at least 300 new installations and obtain 500 new clients by EOY.
- Migrate at least 250 existing clients to Z-TEC web product cost reduction program.
- Increase Gross Margin from 51% to 55% through product cost reduction program.
- Increase sales per field employee from $250,000 to $300,000 this year.
- Reduce Accounts Receivables from 60 days to 45 days.
- Achieve FTE head count of 1,500 by 9/31.

strategies

- Growth: Grow 50% each year by development of new clients and migration of existing clients.
- Reputation: Product position & strong reputation from existing client/partner referrals.
- Partnering: Align with industry leaders, partnering for marketing & solution development.
- Competitive Position: Optimize user/based pricing & modular system concepts for flexibility.
- Product Approach: Configure rather than Customize, Business Rules vs. custom programs.
- R&D: WorkFlow Solutions, Open Systems, multiple environments, Object-Oriented, flexible.
- Develop aligned team, know the plan, have sense of urgency, responsibility & accountability.
- Develop Employee Incentive Program to allow the team to share in the rewards & have fun.

action plans

- Implement Power Partner Initiatives w/Oracle UK by 3/31.
- Complete development of the Z-TEC client/server product by 3/31.
- Develop Sales & Marketing Resource Plan by 3rd Quarter.
- Develop Partner strategies w/PeopleSoft, Sun Micro, IBM by 4/30.
- Launch Europe Customer Forum in London at June Convention.
- Develop Sales Force Automation Plan by August, implement in 4th Quarter.
- Implement financial reporting system at project/dept. level by Oct. 20th.
- Implement professional skills development program by Nov. 15th.

Z-TEC Inc. – Southern European Sales Division

Alex Morgan, Sales Division Mgr.

FY Plan

vision

Within the next three years grow the southern Europe division of Z-TEC into a $150 million business unit with offices in Madrid, Barcelona, Nice and Florence.

mission

Find customers… close contracts!

objectives

- Increase sales to $45 million this year.
- Complete installation of 50 systems this year.
- Increase gross margins from 51 to 55% by increasing sale of value added services.
- Increase contribution margin to $20 million.
- Migrate at least 35 existing clients to Z-TEC internet product by 12/31.
- Reduce accounts receivable from 60 to 45 days.
- Achieve FTE head count of 275 by 9/31.

strategies

- Partners: Align with industry leaders, partnering for marketing & solution development.
- Product Approach: Configure rather than customize business rules vs. custom programs.
- Market Positioning; modular systems for flexibility, customization; premium pricing.
- R&D: Workflow solutions, open systems, multi-platform, object-oriented, flexible.
- Develop an aligned team with sense of urgency, responsibility and accountability.
- Develop employee incentive programs to allow the team to share rewards.

action plans

- Implement Power Partner Initiatives w/Oracle Spain by 7/31.
- Launch European Customer Forum in Spain at June convention.
- Develop Sales Force Automation Plan by 08/31, implement in 4th quarter.
- Implement financial reporting system at project/dept level by 10/31.
- Implement professional skills development program by 11/15.
- Complete Portugal facilities upgrades by 10/31.
- Build communication and team performance among 12 branch managers.

Z-TEC, Inc. – Controller

Gail French, Controller, European Division

Controller's Department Plan

vision

Within the next five years, build an integrated accounting function at Z-TEC that provides complete accounting support services, management & business analysis and budgeting & forecasting to properly support Z-TEC at $2 billion in revenue.

mission

Provide tools & information to manage growth… profitably!

objectives

- Increase gross margins from 38% to 45%.
- Identify and implement $150k in cost saving projects.
- Close and issue monthly financial statements by the 15th of each month by September 30th.
- Reduce Z-TEC accounts receivable from 65 days to 55 days outstanding.
- Pay off line of credit by September 30th..

strategies

- Build a Z-TEC financial services team that can grow with Z-TEC by training/empowerment.
- Build a business mentality by providing training on fin. statements, budgets & forecasting.
- Increase gross profit by creating mgmt. reporting on non-billable time and material.
- Control expense by dept. budgets, use of policy, forecasting system, timely financials.
- Streamline acctg. process w/ operations dept. to minimize month end billing bottlenecks.
- Improve cash flow thru weekly AR collection monitoring and reduce billing errors.
- Streamline the payroll and HR process thru remote data entry and integrated systems.
- Eliminate duplicate data entry/manual reporting by consolidating to one operating system.
- Finance growth thru internal funds and bank debt; control expense/keep margins high.

action plans

- Build initial Financial Reportings, IS, BS, Dept. expense, sales repts. by February 28th.
- Streamline monthly closing procedure by February 28th.
- Train staff in new closing procedure by March 31st; complete job descriptions by April 30th.
- Build Banking System direct deposit to lockbox by Feb 28th.
- Build next year's budget analysis model by August 31st; finalized by September 30th.
- Investigate new payroll system w/HR systems by October 31st.
- Finished next year's budget by Dec 15th.

Z-TEC Inc. – Personnel Manager

Jonee Grassi, Personnel Manager

HR Department Plan

vision

Develop a world class workforce of employees for Z-TEC International and their independent contractors who fuel the growth of the company through their creativity, dedication, and capabilities.

mission

Attract, build and retain a world-class team.

objectives

- Recruit 1,600 new employees by EOY; end year with 3,600 employees.
- Decrease turnover rate from 18% to less than 10%.
- Decrease overtime from 22% to 10% by April 15th.
- Increase average learning program hours/employee to 60 per year.
- Achieve internal promotion rate of 60%.
- Increase flex-scheduling optimization to 90% by September 30th.

strategies

- Hire world-class team players with exceptional skill sets whenever possible.
- Retain our employees by treating them as strategic partners critical to our success.
- Commit to have resources, people & systems in place before they are needed.
- Ensure career development through innovative training & development programs.
- Highly compensate employees for their contribution; generous use of stock options.
- Support work-life balance through flex scheduling and well-being programs.
- Develop Employee Incentive Programs to allow our team to share in the rewards.

action plans

- Implement Z-TEC Employee Hiring Campaign by 01/15.
- Launch Employee Distance Learning Program by 02/01.
- Develop Intranet Flexible Scheduling facility by 04/30; implement by end of Q3.
- Complete national salary survey by 06/30.
- Upgrade Kansas City national training facilities by 06/30.
- Implement professional skills development program by 11/15.

Colorado Garden Window Company

Mike Bozman, CEO

FY Consolidated Plan

vision

Within the next 3 years grow Colorado Garden Window Company into a $40 million national home products company specializing in manufacturing and distributing custom and replacement garden windows and skylights to baby-boomers and home remodelers.

mission

Bring Light, Air, and the Beauty of Nature into homes… through creative windows!

objectives

- Achieve annual sales of $17 million.
- Earn pre-tax profits this year of $1.5 million.
- Target Cost of Goods Sold at 38% of sales.
- Reduce inventory levels to 3.3 months on hand by August 31st.
- Grow Garden Window Division at 8% per year & achieve $5.3M this year.
- Expand skylight/custom window product lines; grow sales to $7.5 million this year.
- Implement profit improvement programs & reduce product costs to 38%.
- Achieve 98% on time delivery with 98% order accuracy by 1st quarter.

strategies

- Focus on new upscale home developments and baby-boomer remodeling trends.
- Build Colorado Garden Window Co. into a nationally recognized brand name.
- Control quality processes by manufacturing solely in-house.
- Become vendor-of-choice by maintaining a constant inventory of standard window sizes.
- Increase capacity & manufacturing efficiency by actively reducing duplicate products.
- Centralize distribution into one location; reducing costs & improving service.

action plans

- Introduce new scenic Garden Window at S.F. products show 3/15.
- Roll out new package design beginning 3/31.
- Expand Sales Dept. to focus on Signature Homes in Denver and Provo by 4/1.
- Introduce inventory reduction program company-wide by 5/1.
- Fully implement new MRP software to achieve inventory reduction by 7/1.
- Complete skylight product rationalization program by 8/15.
- Research, design and roll out re-designed employee benefit program by 10/1.
- Complete product distribution consolidation project by 11/15.

Meals on Wheels

Donna Van Sant, Executive Director

Business Plan Summary

vision

Grow Meals On Wheels program into a premier nutrition service for the home bound elderly and disabled adults in our county, providing a full compliment of quality prepared meals and personal attention seven days a week.

mission

At home and healthy with full nutrition and personal attention.

objectives

- Provide services to 475 home bound elderly each month.
- Provide expanded nutritional service products to 300 individuals.
- Add new customers at the rate of 45 per month by May 1.
- Increase case management revenue to an average of $2,500 per month.
- Recruit and train 25 new route drivers, both volunteer and paid by July 15.
- Obtain $80,000 in county contract and foundation funding by September 30.
- Provide 12 in-service training sessions for route drivers and 24 for MOW staff.
- Provide nutrition services to 75 disabled adults each month.

strategies

- Develop and maintain effective relations with funders; program tours, and proposal writing.
- In conjunction with food services vendors, develop three new products for our customers.
- Develop and execute a customer focused marketing plan for nutrition and CS management.
- Create and execute a staff and volunteer development plan that works!
- Operate our customer feedback and quality control system to increase customer satisfaction.

action plans

- Complete new product development by March 23rd.
- Complete staff hiring and support plan by May 16th.
- Hold program tour and meeting with all current funders by October 10th.
- Win funding from 10 new foundations by November 23rd.
- Develop a marketing plan by December 1st.

City of Pageville Fire Department
Robert Lewellyn, Fire Chief
Consolidated Plan

vision

Within the next three years achieve a fire and emergency services team in the City of Pageville that is characterized by high employee morale and excellent community service.

mission

Elevate citizen confidence that their fire and emergency services are dependable and affordable. Protecting community with quality life… and fire-safety services.

objectives

- Reduce fire response time to 5 minutes average by 12/31.
- Reduce freeway emergency response time to 7 minutes average by 12/31.
- Reduce loss of property by 12% from previous year.
- Assure there is no more than a 5% deviation from last year's monthly overtime budget.
- Reduce worker injuries to no more than 6 per month by 12/31.
- 60% employees involved in participation activities by 7/01.

strategies

- Involve community in neighborhood targeted life and safety program.
- Involve all personnel in every aspect of life and fire safety at their locations.
- Establish and enforce performance based accountability system at all department levels.
- Establish and provide professional growth and opportunity programs for all personnel.
- Coordinate with other agencies to meet emergency response standards.
- Deliver safety education & other services within our mission to the community.
- Aggressively work to prevent hazardous conditions.
- Respond promptly to rescues, fires, medical emergencies and natural disasters.
- Ensure safe, professional, environmentally harmonious actions.

action plans

- Develop a coordinating mechanism to keep track of all elements of the strategic plan by 3/31.
- Accountability systems are developed for all elements of the strategic plan by 6/1.
- Implementation of the strategic plan is monitored on a monthly basis by 7/31.
- Develop a list of comparable cities and fire departments to benchmark our services by 9/1.
- A commitment plan to guide building of a policy maker consensus on service levels by 10/1.
- Implement a comprehensive employee involvement plan by 10/31.
- Implement a comprehensive community involvement plan by 12/31.

Unity of Marin, Spiritual Center

Reverend Richard Mantei

Consolidated Plan

vision

The vision of Unity In Marin is to provide a loving and supportive diverse community which teaches practical Christianity and encourages spiritual growth and action. Within 3 years 700 will attend 3 transformational Sunday services, and a mid-week, and monthly healing service. We will have an active 7-day per week spiritual center and have 100+ children in YE with 40 personal growth and spiritual education class night/events for adults per mo. UIM will have 3 effective outreach programs in Marin County and beyond. People will experience a deep sense of spiritual community, personal transformative growth and service to others as a path to God.

mission

Discover divinity within and reach out in loving service.

objectives

- Increase Sunday attendance from 220 to 400 by July 1.
- Increase annual income from $380,000 to $620,000.
- Increase Y.E. weekly attendance from 15 average to 40 average by March 1.
- Increase new membership from 75 to 100, increase AE class 12 to 25 attend 160 to 450.
- Increase Spring and Fall in-home program from 100/150 to 180/220.
- Increase Service Ministry involvement from 105 to 150.

strategies

- Bld upon successful Sunday Celebration: enhance music & pre/post service experience.
- Meet goals of FIA/CC/LegacyEndow/other profit making events thru excellent in execution.
- Bld Edu. success by increased variety/continuity & excel in curric & teachers.
- Deepen prayer consciousness by expanding role of chaplains, outreach and education.
- Bld membership by better marketing & outreach prog.& congreg. involve.
- Bld upon MLT success by inviting/recognizing/ coaching/thanking excellence in leadership.
- Leverage minister's time by evolving staff and leadership teams.

action plans

- In Q1 Complete negotiations & details for 6 nat'l speakers to appear this year by 1/31.
- In Q1 Complete Sunday, seminar, theme programming for the year by 3/15.
- In Q1 Complete arrangements for once per month healing service.
- In Q2 Finalize plans for a mid-week service to begin in September.
- In Q3 Have 75% of work done in preparation for a Capital Campaign to launch 4/25.
- In Q4 Fully implement transition team for YE leadership by 10/31.
- In Q4 By November 30th, complete plans to implement next year's Capital Campaign.

Bay Area Entrepreneur Association

George Cole, Executive Director

Strategic Plan

vision

Build BAEA into a nationally recognized micro-enterprise organization with an extensive greater San Francisco Bay Area network of entrepreneurial support groups providing nationally recognized products, programs and services to entrepreneurs, small business owners, and partner organizations.

mission

Create viable businesses and successful entrepreneurial leaders through networking, support and connection to resources.

objectives

- Increase membership from 150 to 300 by 12/31.
- Launch 2 networks by the end of this year.
- Generate $8,000 from entrepreneurial programs, events and products in this FY.
- Host 3 regional network events with at least 50 attendees each and generate $3,000.
- Conduct 4 workshops/programs with an average of 25 participants and generate $4,000.
- Increase low-income members to 25 and increase minority members 25% by 3/31.
- Award 5 scholarships totaling $1,300 in this FY.
- Recognize 10 entrepreneurs for outstanding business growth & community service.

strategies

- Use public relations and media to share successes, educate, recruit and fund.
- Market and sell BAEA endorsed products and services nationally.
- Collaborate with nat'l micro-enterprise org. in nat'l awareness programs and funding.
- Establish BAEA center to create long-term community presence & financial asset base.
- Enlist key community leaders and businesses to launch and develop new networks.
- Attract/retain low-income entrepreneurs by offering scholarships funded by corp. sponsors.
- Utilize multi-lingual/cultural programs to attract minority entrepreneurs.
- Package successful BAEA programs & products to sell to other micro-enterprise orgs.
- Use technology to manage growth, streamline ops., and deliver programs, & sell products.

action plans

- Complete 5-year Strategic Plan by 6/20.
- Complete funding plan by 6/201. Raise $100,000 by 11/20.
- Hire executive director by 11/20.
- Expand board of directors from 4 to 7 by 10/2.
- Develop BAEA product and service marketing plan by 8/20.
- Develop 2-year network expansion plan by 5/25.
- Launch sales/marketing plan of One Page Business Plan by 6/30.
- Collect and write 20 success stories by 7/20; Implement PR Plan by 8/31.

Portland Insurance Agency

Consolidated Agency Plan

vision

Within the next three years grow the Greater Portland Insurance Agency into a $15 million agency system with three locations providing auto, property & casualty, life insurance and financial services to individuals, families and businesses that are concerned about being protected from the unpleasant and unexpected events of life.

mission

Prepare and Protect the Families and Businesses in our community!

objectives

- Increase total revenue from $8 to $10 million this year.
- Add 2,000 new policies this year generating $1.2 million in incremental revenue.
- Increase average annual premium from $500 to $550.
- Increase client retention rate from 88.35% to 91%.
- Increase # of average appointments per agent from 1.9 to 5 per week by April 30th.
- Increase close rate from 25% to 50% by June 30th.
- Increase life insurance referrals from 2 to 5 per week per agent.
- Hire 5 new agents by April 1st, additional 7 new agents by October 1st.

strategies

- Become locally known for excellence in "family & business insurance solutions".
- Build long term relationships w/ prominent bus. leaders - create consistent referral source.
- Maximize visibility by serving on community, non-profit, & professional boards.
- Mine existing client base for "A" clients; use seminar marketing system to find "B"clients.
- Strategic Mkting Alliances - align w/ CPA's, attorneys, auto dealers, real estate professionals.
- Sell thru education; use computer presentations to assure consistent message delivery.
- Staffing - hire professionals, provide quality training, 1:1 mentoring, reward Winners.
- Streamline all internal support & admin functions thru effective & smart use of technology.

action plans

- Implement agent incentive reward plan Jan. 15th.
- Kickoff new agent search/hire process Feb. 1st; Training to begin April 15th.
- Contribute 1 article/month to Oregonian & Portland Tribune newspapers beginning Feb. 1st.
- Develop strat. relationship/Coop mktg program w/ major CPA firm & Law firm beg. 5/1.
- Conduct Credit Union member estate planning workshops every 8 weeks starting July 1st.
- Launch "Help a Non-Profit" initiative Sept. 30th.
- Re-launch High School Financial Program Oct. 1st.
- Move to new Portland Financial Center Nov. 1st.

Esteem Music Academy

Mary Walby, Founder, Senior Piano Instructor

Business Plan

vision

Within the next year grow Esteem Music Academy into an in-demand Western Whatcom County piano school providing private and group piano instruction, from novice to intermediate level, performance, technique, and theory education, concerts, and team and life building skills, ages 7 to 10, accompany church services, receptions and weddings with $75K sales.

mission

Experiencing fun playing music and building confidence.

objectives

- Achieve sales of 75K this year.
- Hire 4 p/t employees/consultants by Jan 15th.
- Add 17 new clients; 7 by Feb 15th, 10 by May 15th.
- Increase number of concerts from 1 to 2 per month by Aptil 1st.
- Increase from 1 to 2 number of music teachers by June 1st.
- Develop a Strategic Alliance Program with 8 members by Aug 15th.
- Increase hourly rate to $60 by Sept 30th.
- Create Esteem Music Method by Oct 1st.

strategies

- Focus on children ages 7-10 and beginners.
- Become regionally known as a music school that provides life skills.
- Focus on training grammar schools in affluent neighborhoods.
- Core products/services are 1:1 music classes, group sessions, and accompaniments.
- Promote initial trial of Practice Cards for students AND Esteem Cards for their parents.
- Pricing strategy is value-based, develop marketing funnel and increase rates.
- Hire bookkeeper, music teacher, administrative person, and house cleaner.
- Use technology to market online, automate/streamline systems, develop future curriculum.
- Create processes for hiring, operations manual, and framework for curriculum.

action plans

- Develop Pricing Structure (Jan).
- Create client intake process (Jan).
- Build blog or Wiki for curriculum development (Mar).
- Schedule 4 speaking events and 2 concerts (Mar).
- Develop company brand by June 1st.
- Hire 4 employees/consultants by Aug 15th.
- Expand internet presence w/shopping cart by Oct 15th.
- Develop 2 products by Nov 15th.
- Create operations manual by Dec 31st.

Christina Ecklund Design

Christina Iantorano, Owner

Business Plan

---

vision

Within the next 3-5 years grow Christina Ecklund Design into a $500,000 national fashion jewelry business providing unique trend and classic jewelry and fashion accessories to women ages 24 - 50, who want to be unique but not spend a fortune ($60 - $145). Each piece is designed and hand crafted in the USA.

---

mission

Create stunning jewelry and accessories that are as unique and special as the women who wear them.

---

objectives

- Achieve FY sales of $24,000.
- Earn pre-tax profits of $12,000.
- Add 20 new accounts; 10 in 1st half, 10 in 2nd half.
- Increase average sale from $60 to $400. Encourage multiples in ordering.
- Increase repeat purchase rate from 50% to 95%.
- Send out product samples to stores and contact for feed back or order.
- Sell 200 units of jewelry at average price of $120.
- Deliver 100% of orders (all made to order in the 1st & 2nd quarter) on time.

---

strategies

- Focus on wholesale & retail markets. Find retailers specifically geared to my target.
- Attract/solicit new wholesale buyers & retail customers.
- Focus on trade show, direct store marketing & fashion trends. Get my name out there.
- Core Product is unique well priced designer jewelry and accessories.
- Our pricing strategy is keep prices in the mid range, focus on multiple sales.
- Encourage repeat purchases by offering new products on a regular basis.
- Create website where people can shop my products as well as link to stores.
- Increase awareness in the market with periodicals, working with buyers & trade shows.
- Grow business at 10% per year by adding new products, new divisions & promotions.

---

action plans

- Hire a small work force to fabricate my designs and fill orders by Jan 15th.
- Create internal shipping department by April 15th.
- Show line at Los Angeles gift show in Sept.
- Create web site with shopping capabilities to increase revenue by Aug 15th.
- Display at Las Vegas Fashion Magic show Oct 5-7.
- Introduce Fancy Bird Studio (Teen Line) by Oct 1st.
- Hire and streamline work force using outside labor sources by Nov 15th.
- Design and fabricate Spring Line to present at Gift Show San Francisco in Aug.

Eti-Kits

Sharyn Amoroso, Owner

Business Plan

vision

Within the next 3 years grow Eti-Kits into a $1 million company through sales of booklets, DVD's, and accessories. Establish brand recognition so that "Eti-Kits" becomes synonymous with the essential tools and guides needed to learn good manners in today's world, while positioning myself as the new spokesperson for etiquette.

mission

Bring the ease of learning good manners to anyone.
Simplifying what people need to know to be their best!

objectives

- Achieve anuual gross sales of $90,000 in customized booklets.
- Increase internet sales of products to $10,000.
- Reduce credit line balance and loans to less than $10,000 by year end.
- Add 15 corporate accounts for bulk orders of booklets generating $6,000 each by Jan 30th.
- Sell Eti-Kits line of products to major corporation for $5 million within 5 years.
- Generate $5,000/month in speaker fees starting June 30th.

strategies

- Core products are etiquette mini-guides, DVD's, Napkin Clips, accessories.
- National pitch with different angles for various markets timed with seasonal issues.
- Target broad base of clients to determine where interest and sales translate best.
- Methodically grow "Eti-Kits" name recognition by PR printed media, TV, internet.
- Raise my nat'l profile as leading etiquette spokesperson via news, mags, TV, internet.
- Focus on parenting, higher education, and business professional markets.
- Pursue HR Depts of major corporations for sales of mini-guides for employees.
- Continue personal education in the field of social, business, and military etiquette.

action plans

- Hire intern to sell mini-guides to HR Depts. w/1,000 employees by 1/15.
- Hire PR to launch blitz of Napkin Clips to parenting & family markets by 2/15.
- Expand internet exposure and sales via Amazon, Facebook, LinkedIn, PSOW by 3/15.
- PR to blitz Napkin Clips to food & travel, senior & special needs markets by 6/1.
- Complete first draft of Children's mini-guide by 8/15.
- Plan production of Dining DVD with videographer by 9/15.
- PR to establish Sharyn as expert spokesperson to TV & print media by year end.

Film Studio
Gladys Deniz, Executive Director
Business Plan

ONE
PAGE
PLAN

vision

Within the next 3 years build a non-profit sound stage film studio and screen play/stage theater for local high school students in Fresno county with an annual funding goal of $150,000.

mission

We help high school students share their life story on film.

objectives

- Raise initial $250,000 capital to build a sound stage film studio by Jan 31st.
- Generate $150,000 on-going operating budget for student film productions annually.
- Recruit 100 liberal arts students into 4-year film study program by March 31st.
- Achieve 100% participation of film students in annual Slick Rock film festival.
- Place 70% of students into summer film workshops at SF Academy of Arts.
- Evaluate program goals with student pre-eval (Sept) and post-eval (June) annually.

strategies

- Hold informational film study program meetings with local 8th grade students.
- Increase awareness of student films with production screenings at local theaters.
- Focus on YouTube & Internet trends for student film distribution opportunities.
- Hold fundraisers at local film theaters selling 250 Wall of Fame bricks for $100 ea.
- Focus on 15 high-end local film producers to rent studio 10 days/yr @ $1,000/day.
- Invest in HD & 3D technology to attract local film producer investors.
- Research state and federal grant funding opportunities & solicit donor support.

action plans

- Partner w/Washington High School to add film production to their academy by Jan 15th.
- Hire project manager to secure grant funding and construction proposals by 3/15.
- Visit bay area high schools with film production studios for construction ideas by 4/30.
- Consult w/ Stephen Burum regarding equipping student sound stages, July.
- Announce studio project at fall conference of Fresno Filmmakers Alliance, Oct.
- Complete design plan for studio construction by 12/31.

Pam Hutchinson, Realtor

Pam Hutchinson, Owner

Business Plan

vision

Within the next 2 years grow Pam Hutchinson, Realtor into a $ 20,000 comprehensive, customer-oriented real estate business in the Middle Tennessee area providing exceptional customer service, including access to multiple MLS search capabilities, to individuals and families either buying or selling commercial or residential property in Dover, TN and surrounding areas.

mission

Moving up or just moving on… everyone's a winner

objectives

- Increase revenue from $1,600 to $20,000.
- Raise pre-tax profits from a loss of $6,300 to a profit of $15,000.
- Decrease annual percentage of unsold listed properties from 50% to 33%.
- Boost average annual listings from 6 to 12; one per month.
- Increase average monthly growth of prospect list from 1 to 3.
- Increase annual trips to visit family/friends from 2 to 3.
- Reduce # of training hours from 100 to 20.
- Decrease avg work week from 7 days to 3 days.

strategies

- Assure excel cust svc w/ timely follow-up, excpt prod knowl base and lots of hustle.
- Use Internet/Tech to communicate with clients, maintain records and mkt business.
- Mkt bus by local networking, local advertising and high qual print & electr materials
- Focus business with OPBP, on-going bus coaching and giving up second job.
- Build aware of local prop w/ rev of daily updates, reg prop previews and pers contact.
- Prom prof growth w/ cont CEU's, reading prof journals, internet rsrch & peer trng.
- Prov self care w/ trips to see fam/friends, no 2nd job, & more qual time w/spouse.
- Assure profit by incr prspt client base, reduc expen and creating passive inc sources
- Control expenses by reduc trng, reduc/reuse/recycle, smart choices & peer bulk prch.

action plans

- Implement Updated Marketing Plan by March 15.
- Launch Knowledge Base Improvement Program by March 31.
- Hire Business Coach by May 1.
- Build at least one source of Passive Income by June 1.
- Launch Family and Friends Travel Plan by June 30.
- Complete Technology Update by July 1.
- Launch new Web Site by August 1.
- Complete first phase of Biz Focus Project by October 1.
- Complete Limited Annual Training Plan by November 30.

Tri-Valley Financial Advisory Services

George Rask, CFP

vision

By year-end, grow George Rask, at Tri-Valley Advisory Services, into a $350,000 financial advisory service practice managing 40,000,000 in assets, providing trusted financial planning to 30 to 60 year-old clients for their retirement, and for their family's future wealth, who live in the greater Phoenix metro area.

mission

We help families provide for their families!

objectives

- Achieve annaul production growth of 33%, growing from $150,000 to $200,000.
- Boost return on assets from 0.20% to 0.40%.
- Increase assets from $21 million to $28 million.
- Maintain the same number accounts while culling lowest 10% of accounts from my BOB.
- Achieve asset-based revenue of 70% of BOB.
- Decrease transaction-based revenue from 38% to 30%.

strategies

- Focus on executing plan, frequent client contact, reviewing markets & client data.
- Capitalize on current clients, and planning and development of trends/opportunities.
- Attract new clients by consistently soliciting referrals in current BOB.
- Positive daily actions are focusing on contacts with clients, reduce administrivia.
- Increase face time with personalized mail campaigns, notes & flawless follow-up.
- Gather AUM by returning to my entire client list for additional assets each quarter.
- Grow assets by closing top 10 referral prospects I have on a monthly basis.

action plans

- Cull 10% of my accounts 2/15.
- Complete retraining on Financial Planning (CFP exam) by 3/15.
- Employ regular use of BIS beginning no later than 4/15.
- Utilize "Financial Planning System" for my top 10% clients beginning 6/15.
- Perform mid-year course correction, and revise business plan as necessary by 6/30.

Family Wealth Counselors, Inc.

Allen Johnson, Financial Advisor

vision

Within the next three years grow Allen Johnson, Financial Advisor at Family Wealth Counselors to $75,000,000 in Assets Under Management, with revenues of $700,000 by providing consultative financial services in the greater San Diego area to truly compatible clients consisting of busy professionals, active retirees, non-profit organizations and small to medium businesses.

mission

Take complexity out of family wealth.

objectives

- Increase gross revenue from $207,000 to $315,000.
- Grow AUM from $32.7 million to $45 million.
- Boost my ROA from .59 to .70 BPS.
- Eliminate all $0-$35k households clients by 6/30.
- Expand +$100k households clients from 51 to 80.

strategies

- Focus on small business retirement, non-profit endowment & high net worth markets.
- Attract/solicit high net worth thru golf club, non-profit and close personal network.
- Minimize account transfer threats by improved customer service & relationship mgmt.
- Utilize sales and marketing asst. to boost business; increase face time, improve image.
- Pattern business after successful Financial Advisors thru study/observation/interaction.
- Attract new clients thru mail and calling campaigns and persistent follow-up.

action plans

- Complete training and implementation of SMART! database for myself and CSA by EOY.
- Launch 2 aggressive campaigns per quarter to clients and prospects alike.
- Close 6 small biz retirement plans at rate of 1 every other month; beg. 1/15
- Hold 5 successful golf events for clients; May, June, July, Aug, Sept.
- Complete 12 non-profit endowment presentations by 6/15. 12 more by 12/15.
- Hold weekly Rookie FA business planning meetings for this branch; beg 5/1.

Tulsa Risk & Insurance Services

Susan McNalley

Four Month Plan

ONE
PAGE
PLAN

---

vision

In the next four months (Sept - Dec) grow my Tulsa PCS practice into a $12K/month revenue generating business specializing in personal P&C sales to high net worth individuals.

---

mission

Create peace of mind through proactive personal risk management.

---

objectives

- Achieve FY sales of $100,000.
- Work with prospects greater than or equal to $15K ICP 90% of the time.
- Call 35 prospects by Oct 31st.
- Implement suspect COI strategy w/ 114 suspect COIs in my database 12/1.
- Produce minimum of $12K in revenue every month his year.

---

strategies

- Leverage client and COI relationships for new business referrals to ICP prospects.
- Est. performance team via execution & accountability w/ AEs, Stews, MAA, & Claims.
- Develop suspect COIs w/Coninuous Contact COI Strategy Plan (CCCOISP)
- Grow business by asking for & working w/ICP clients.
- Ask every suspect COI for "test case or diagnostic" app w/ their clientele.
- Use direct mail for access to Top 50 prospects and large homes in target market.
- Confirm value and ask for referrals from clients at every meeting.
- Follow up w/ AE and Prospects on open cases weekly.
- Put all suspect COIs thru CCCOISP.

---

action plans

- Direct mail to large SGV homes by 9/30.
- Client-Confirm Value: ask 4 referrals 2 prospects/COIs.
- Mail letters and f-u by phone to Top 50 by Oct 15th.
- Mail /in-person (CCCOISP) 6 to 7 pre-determined items throughout year based on A, B, or C.
- Dial 75 suspect COIs by Nov 15th.

McKenzie Estate Planning Associates

Bob McKenzie

Consolidated Plan

vision

Become premiere mid-tier estate planning attorney in Central Valley Counties with offices in Sacramento and Fresno operating in collaboration with selected law firms, CPAs, Life Insurance Agents, Stock Brokers, and other Financial Advisors.

mission

We help create, preserve and utilize family wealth for important social causes.

objectives

- Produce annual gross of $480,000 and net of $240,000.
- Be retained by two new clients a month at average fee of $20K each.
- Conduct 10 class sessions by 6/31 with average attendance of 10 prof @ $25 each.
- Conduct 40 class sessions in 12/15 with average attendance of 10 prof @ $25 each.
- Co-conduct 2 seminars by 12/31 with CPA's clients on Advanced Est Plan.
- Co-conduct 4 seminars by 12/31 with CPA's clients on Advanced Est Plan.
- Obtain 4 qualified Ad Est Plan referrals from Profs with conversion ratio of 50%.
- Obtain 1 qualified Ad Est Plan referral from clients with conversion ratio of 50%.
- Maintain $150,000/year of existing client base practice.

strategies

- Specialize in estate planning design, legal docs & services to persons of over $1 mil net worth.
- Provide training to CPAs, attorneys, financial advisors & life insurance agents.
- Restrict Bob McKenzie to professional services and delegate office operations.
- Obtain services of marketing person to sign up professionals for classes.
- Attend professional programs to be up-to-date in field.
- Use technology to maintain both offices & deliver state-of-art estate plans & documents.
- Attract and retain key employees by paying above average and bonus.

action plans

- Develop CPA Est & Gift Tax class-get it approved for CE 8 hrs credit by 8/31.
- Teach 2 CPA Est Plan classes by 11/30.
- Get Life Ins Est Plan class reapproved CE credit for 10 hours by 9/30.
- Teach 2 Life Ins Est Plan classes by 12/15.
- Develop Est Planning Mktg 4 hour class for Fin Advisors by 10/30.
- Teach 2 attorney classes by 12/15.
- Develop Est & Gift Tax class for attys by 10/30.
- Teach 2 attorney classes by 12/15.

Oklahoma Jazz Hall of Fame

Chuck Cissel

Executive Director

vision

Within the next three years, grow the Oklahoma Jazz Hall of Fame into an international art institution with annual funding of $1.3 million, providing preservation, education and performance of jazz to music lovers.

mission

Creating Unity Through Music

objectives

- Increase Revenue from $434,947 to $500,000.
- Increase Surplus from $44,878 to $55,000.
- Increase membership from 400 to 600.
- Increase performances revenue from $77,000 to $123,000.
- Increase donations from $374,884 to $750,000.
- Increase grants from $259,784 to $520,000.
- Increase educational program from 3 to 5 & scholarships from four to eight.
- Increase staff from 2 to 6.
- Increase volunteers from 15 to 50.

strategies

- Increase revenues and surplus by promoting performances, galas & space rental.
- Build/attract membership base by promotion, advertising & organization.
- Increase performance rev. by offering diverse programming, increasing frequency & mktg.
- Build donations by dev a capital campaign plan, hiring a dev consultant and a grant writer.
- Engage and educate youth by use of library, computers & practices.
- Expand scholarship endowment by corporate & individual donations & grants.
- Improve Board eff. by targeted recruiting, pre-evaluation & involvement through planning.
- Hire world-class staff by developing specific job descs, for key staff, recruiting and selection.
- Attract/retain volunteer base by membership, marketing & external programs.

action plans

- CC-Complete HR systems job descriptions by 02/28.
- JH-Establish scholarship selection committee by 3/31.
- HS-Roll out volunteer/membership committee by 3/31.
- JJ-Report on Board membership committee by 3/31.
- JH-Dev education committee w/staff member in charge of educational programs by 3/31.
- LS- Dev feasibility study by 5/31.
- CC-Recruit & hire additional staff by 07/31.
- CC-Implement the financial plan to achieve revenue & surplus by 09/30.

Burlingame Library Foundation

Stephen Hamilton

President

vision

Over the next 3 years Burlingame Library Foundation will provide the Burlingame Library with a reliable income stream of $250k per year through fund raising activities, events and endowment programs. These funds will be dedicated to the Burlingame Library for the purpose of supporting programs, infrastructure, and other activities that would not otherwise be funded or supported via the annual library budget.

mission

Ensuring and enhancing the library's role in our community.

objectives

- Increase active donor list to 500/year by 6/31.
- Increase average donation to $500/year by 8/31.
- Increase active contact list to 5,000 by 10/1.
- Create endowment asset base of $1M by 12/31.
- Increase # of fund raising activities (book sales, newsletters, events) to 6/year by 12/31.
- Reduce donor attrition to < 10% per year by 12/31.

strategies

- Inc. the visibility of the library foundation through communications, events and ambassadors.
- Create a donor community through repeatable events and activities.
- Create reliable income stream through planned giving and endowments.
- Develop an ongoing communication program for all past donors.
- Communicate regularly with all foundation service users (story hours, book clubs etc).
- Increase awareness of foundation with key influencing groups

action plans

- Launch website and e-communications by July 1.
- Create plan for events for next 24 months by July 30.
- Investigate and establish planned giving program by Sept 30.
- Create complete donor analysis by Sept 30.
- Re-establish links with advisory committee and trustees by Oct 1.
- Communicate with all past & present donors by Oct 31.
- Update all foundation publicity materials by Jan 1.
- Create communication program for all user groups (newcomers, young parents etc) by Feb 1.
- Align board / committee responsibilities by March 1.

THE ONE PAGE BUSINESS PLAN

Center on Juvenile & Criminal Justice

Dan Macallair

Executive Director

vision

To become the leading organization in the nation on alternatives to incarceration and criminal justice reform by:
- Developing high quality innovative program models.
- Conducting and disseminating high-level policy analysis and research.
- Providing technical assistance to government and nonprofit agencies.
- Developing comprehensive public education strategies.
- Establishing a network of affiliated agencies.

mission

To reduce society's use of incarceration as a solution to social problems.

objectives

- Raise a minimum of $50,000 for new initiatives by July 31.
- Host two conferences in Sept, funded by foundations to generate $50,000.
- Establish a minimum cash reserve of $30,000 by September 30.
- Cut monthly operating expenses by $10,000 per month by June 30.
- Increase agency revenue by 15% in this fiscal year from $2.0 to $2.3 million.
- Reduce CJCJ's long-term liabilities by 50% from $500,000 to $250,000 by June 30.
- Add one new long-term sustainable program generating $250k a year by Sept. 30.
- Establish a line of credit between $50,000 and $100,000 by December 31.

strategies

- Immediately reduce all unnecessary expenses, establish frugal mind-set.
- Critically review all staffing positions; selectively eliminate; stay lean.
- Establish much tighter control of contracts, invoicing and collections.
- Negotiate advances on existing and new contracts by asking for more money up front.
- Upgrade accounting staff and systems with assistance of non-profit accounting experts.
- Leverage Board member relationships to negotiate settlements of long term liabilities.
- Expand outreach to long term funders, develop new initiatives to increase revenue.
- Increase individual donor base w/ solicitation letters; use donor list from friends & allies.
- Ensure sustainability by improved program effectiveness & more fee for service work.

action plans

- Complete create overall business recovery plan w/ Board by Jan 1.
- Initiate fund raising outreach to foundations by March 1.
- Complete process evaluations for all direct service programs by June 30.
- Complete internal audit by July 31 to determine expense reduction opportunities.
- Engage Briones International to manage accounting systems crisis starting 7/1.
- Negotiate with nonprofit loan agencies to establish line of credit by Sept. 15.
- Fully implement a new accounting system by Oct 31.
- Rebuild website to facilitate online fund raising; complete design 11/10; install 12/1.

Alzheimer's Care Clinic

Kim Newton
Executive Director

vision

Build a spectrum of quality community-based services for the elderly from senior centers to Alzheimer care.

mission

Provide supportive services for the elderly and their families that maximize independence and dignity.

objectives

- Provide services to 350 individuals who have Alzheimer's or a related dementia.
- Provide case management services to 180 individuals in Tri-County area.
- Provide Ombudsman services in Tri-County; 4,800 contacts with residents.
- Operate the Tri-County Adult Day Support Center at 35 average daily census.
- Operate the Metro Adult Day Support Center at 26 average daily census.
- Serve 110,000 meals through the Meals on Wheels Program.
- Serve 1,000 seniors through the OMI Senior Center.
- Increase fee-for-service revenue to $525,000; 25% above last year.
- Obtain additional $125,000 in Foundation funding.

strategies

- Develop and execute a marketing plan that effectively increases revenue from fees.
- Renew contracts with Madison and Perkins counties at 5% increase funding.
- Provide motivation and support to Program Directors to increase performance.
- Obtain greater support from foundations and other donors.
- Develop a knowledge management process for internal and external best practices.

action plans

- Create a marketing plan by Jan. 31st and implement immediately.
- Develop proposals for County contracts by Feb. 15th.
- Submit 3 new proposals to 9 Tri-County Foundations by May 31st.
- Develop and implement a staff motivation plan by Aug. 31st, includes bonus & prof. dev.
- Meet with key funders at least once every 6 months; first meeting Sept. 20th.

The Wellspring

Judy Bell

CEO

ONE
PAGE
PLAN

vision

Within 5 years we see ourselves as the premier Family Service Agency and the charity of choice among local, regional, state and national stakeholders. They have a clear understanding of who we are and what we do. We see a growing funding base to include a $500,000 endowment and an operating reserve of 3-6 months supported by entrepreneurial revenue generating programs to yield a more diversified and flexible funding base. We will be recognized as the "The Can Do Will Do" organization.

mission

To strengthen and value the family through direct service, education, advocacy, and women's leadership

objectives

- To increase total number of new clients by 10% annually
- Identify new funding sources yielding an increase of 3-5% funding annually
- Increase awareness of organizational brand to 50%
- Maintain involuntary turnover rate of employees at less than 15% annually
- Increase volunteer hours to 6000 annually.
- Maintain ratio of revenue to FTE's at less than $70,000
- Maintain staff satisfaction rates on a scale of 1-5 at a minimum of 4.25
- Increase in kind donations by 20% annually

strategies

- Outcome based programming based on a compelling mission and strong core values
- Maintain cost effective, accountable efficient business operations with high integrity
- Enhance diversified and sustainable funding plan including an endowment fund
- Demonstrate a bias for marketing
- Engage in long range planning that responds to community needs and trends
- Be known as employer of choice in community with committed, caring, competent staff
- Engage in strong collaboration and alliance activities
- Maintain state of the art facilities and equipment in multiple locations
- Ensure that program participants are demographically reflective of the community.

action plans

- Implement Marketing Plan & Fund Dev. plans by Dec. 31.
- Recertification of LANO Standards of Excellence by Dec. 15.
- Review/revise Agency Strategic Plan by August 31.
- Reorganize and conduct "Celebrate the Family" fund/friend raiser by June.
- Develop plans for 100th birthdays and 75th anniversary by August.
- Develop endowment program by Dec. 31.
- Complete repairs to Hall House by Dec. 31.
- Update and/or establish policies that support programs/agency by Sept 30.
- Review/Revise Employee Benefit Plan including salary ranges, etc. by Sept. 30.

Shea Therapeutic Equestrian Center

Dana Butler-Moburg

Executive Director

---

vision

With the next three years, grow the Shea Center into a preeminent $2 million organization providing therapeutic equestrian activities to a diverse community of people with special needs, and providing internationally recognized education to therapeutic equestrian professionals.

---

mission

Improving the lives of people with disabilities through therapeutic horse-related programs.

---

objectives

- Expand operating campaign to $1.7 Million.
- Raise $1.5 Million through capital campaign.
- Increase annual fund to $250,000.
- Implement bi-lingual programming with 12 families.
- Increase community awareness by 50%.
- Raise $500,000 by June 30 through Campaign Committee leadership.

---

strategies

- Core services include therapeutic riding, hippotherapy, and non-mounted activities.
- Raise capital funds using new campaign committee.
- Redesign and staff annual fund and face-face giving program.
- Increase public awareness through community speaking and media relations.
- Develop campaign prospects through new Board connections.
- Maintain development focus thru weekly review mtgs.
- Develop more effective budget, cost control, reporting systems.
- Dana to be more involved in developing prospects, solicitation and stewardship.

---

action plans

- Hire new business manager to take on operational responsibilities.
- Recreate Campaign Committee by June 30.
- Recruit 5 Comm members (8/31), ID prospect list (9/30), develop new materials (9/30)
- Develop community speaking program (6/30). Deliver monthly talks in Fall.
- Staff Board, all Committees (6/30). Board Training (Sept)
- Begin monthly development meetings (6/15); bi-weekly (9/15).
- Track all objectives through monthly report (6/15)
- Complete equestrian facility (7/31), offices (11/30).

Management Development Program

Jerome Johnson

CEO

vision

Evolve the existing management team into a vital growing force that:
- Fuels the growth of the foundation by seeing and being a part of the larger vision.
- Builds on its own energy and successes; and learns from its failures/shortfalls.
- Expands its capacity to contribute to the overall management of the organization.
- Develops an esprit de corps that is supportive of the individual, the team, and the organization.
- Develops a service-oriented team focused on meeting the needs of our clients.
- Designs a flexible & adaptable work style/culture able to move quickly & profitably.

mission

Build a management team that builds the business!

objectives

- Improve quality of decision making (measurement TBD).
- Decrease amt. of time & effort to achieve mgmt. buy-in on key projects (measurement TBD).
- Reduce average time in management meetings from 25 hours/month to 12.
- Reduce average work week for management from 60 hours to 45 hours.
- Increase internal promotion ratio from 5% to 25%.
- Decrease management turnover from 20% per year to 5%.

strategies

- Evolve the management team over time; do not go for immediate quick fix.
- Encourage growth and increased participation, geared to individual learning styles.
- Transfer skills from President to the mgmt. staff; provide training and coaching as needed.
- Raise collective business and financial consciousness of the team by the sharing of info.
- Allow for small errors, learn from all mistakes, and celebrate the successes!
- Minimize fanfare about the process; let team respond to positive, subtle changes.

action plans

- Implement business planning and budgeting process for his year starting in Nov.
- Design and implement financial reporting system at "level 2" by Jan. 31.
- Implement monthly business review sessions starting Feb. 20.
- Use CGC Consulting Group to facilitate quarterly "development meetings" starting March 15.
- Implement new manager's training program in June; new supervisor's training in Aug.
- Begin development of new employee orientation learning module starting Oct 1.
- Complete development of new employee orientation learning module in Dec. 31.

Pacific Center

Juan Barajas
Executive Director

vision

Within 3 years, grow Pacific Center into a $650,000 sustainable non-profit organization offering a wide variety of human services to the East Bay LGBT community while providing strong leadership and becoming visible as THE community and media voice so all LGBT people ultimately have a place at the table.

mission

Connecting the LGBT Community in the East Bay!

objectives

- Secure $139,500 in foundation grants by 4/1.
- Earn $90,000 in clinic revenues by 6/30.
- Raise $67,500 in individual donations by 6/30.
- Reduce overhead costs by 10%, from $81,000 to $73,000 by 6/30.
- Increase # of POC clients from 40% to 50% by 6/30.
- Increase # of transgender clients from 10% to 15% by 6/30.
- Increase # of senior clients from 10% to 15% by 6/30.

strategies

- Become the leading voice & media resource of the SF East Bay LGBT community.
- Create a culture of creativity, forward-motion, and partnership with all stakeholders.
- Grow Pacific Center w/ a fundraising board, increasing PR, & developing new programs.
- Dev. strong relationships w/ key leaders thru mtgs., attending commty events, & networking.
- Inc. client diversity thru outreach to target groups, improved language capacity, & staff trng.
- Improve svcs. thru program integration, offsite delivery, & effective client feedback system.
- Strengthen clinic through more eff. screening, improve client tracking, & intern supervision.
- Connect w/ media by regular press releases, dev reporter relationships, & ptnr w/ GLAAD.
- Increase staff capacity through new intern positions, volunteer recruitment, & mgt training.

action plans

- Attract & place new program, development, and communications interns by 10/1.
- Implement donor acquisition, cultivation, & appreciation program by 10/1.
- Initiate organizational creativity & collaboration culture shift by 10/1.
- Fully implement diversity outreach and service capability by 11/1.
- Complete overhead reduction project by 2/1.
- Roll out service improvement project with 1 new offsite service location by 2/15.
- Secure one new STRATEGIC service, advocacy, overhead reduction partnership by 3/1.
- Complete board recruitment by 4/1.
- Run 3 Bay Area media stories by 5/1.

Just Say Yes - Educational Technology Foundation

Robert Chew

Executive Director

ONE
PAGE
PLAN

vision

Our vision is to build Just Say Yes into a international educational technology foundation that supports, encourages and fosters America's Young Entrepreneurial Spirit.
Just Say Yes programs will include:
• Virtual University" (How To Do Business On The Internet).
• International One Page Business Plan™ Contest for students.
• Television Programs featuring Young Internet Entrepreneurs.
• Virtual Mentor Video Conferencing Network

mission

Educate, equip, support, and train "Young" Internet based entrepreneurs.

objectives

• Launch initial One Page Bus. Plan Contest by Feb. 15th & produce 25 winners by 12/31.
• Establish 100 Internet Entrepreneur Clubs in 10 key cities by June 15th; 200 by 12/31.
• Enroll 1,000 students in "Virtual Mentor" program by July 1st & 2,500 by Nov. 1st.
• Create 250 "Virtual Designer" Design Teams by Sept. 15th.
• Host 500 student Internet biz web sites by 2/1, 2,000 by 6/30& 5,000 by 12/31.
• Capitalize Just Say Yes w/ $1,000,000 in donations, sponsorships & pledges by 10/31.

strategies

• Identify most successful Internet entrepreneurs thru fun One Page Bus. Plan™ contests.
• Teach students to write Internet biz plans, design sites, & conduct profitable e-commerce
• Extensively use video conferencing to mentor, train, recognize and foster YES spirit.
• Establish Internet Entrepreneur Clubs at high schools, colleges, youth clubs & org.
• Build "Just Say YES" into an int'l brand name at high schools & colleges worldwide.
• Fund foundation thru donations, corp. sponsors, product sales, Internet stock options.
• Provide inexpensive turn-key business web sites equipped with e-commerce

action plans

• Complete recruitment of 100 member Board of Advisors by 4/30. 200 by 11/30.
• Complete formal business plan & funding development program by April 15th.
• Develop C.D. and Video on "One Page Business Plan" for the Internet by June 1st
• Create "Virtual Mentor" Video Conferencing Network for students by July 15th.
• Equip 25 successful Internet Entrepreneurs w/ Video Conferencing Cameras by 9/1.
• Develop/Produce Young Internet Entrepreneur Video Conferencing Directories by 10/1.
• Launch "Sponsor A Young Internet Entrepreneur" on Radio and T.V. by Nov. 15th.

Notes

Final Thought...

Most of us have no shortage of good ideas! The issue is which ideas are we going to act on?

Learn how to say no to "good ideas"... yours, your partners, employees, associates, friends and family. You only have time, money and resources to execute against the "great ideas." The great ideas can be written on the back of an envelope. They are memorable! They catalyze people and businesses.

Planning doesn't need to be complex! Keep it simple!

Jim Horan
President
The One Page Business Plan Company

Sell More Consulting with One Page Plans!

A Proven, Profitable & Unique Deliverable

Over the last twenty years over 600 certified One Page consultants have implemented The One Page Business Plan® system in thousands of mid-market companies, sales organizations, non-profits and divisions of Fortune 500 companies around the world.

One Page engagements with management teams can range from $5,000 to $50,000 or more! Annual renewals and continuing fees provide steady revenue for your firm from an ever-growing client base.

- Unique cloud-based planning system attracts new clients
- Solid deliverables lead to larger consulting engagements
- Improve client retention, creates residual income
- Ongoing marketing and sales support
- Recognized global brand

Join our consulting team! As a licensee, you will:

Increase the visibility of your firm with our global brand.
Have a powerful prospecting tool with a high conversion rate.
Produce significant and demonstrable results for your clients... quickly!
Have access to state-of-the-art cloud-based software that is available only through our licensees.
Client acquisition is significantly easier with a proven portfolio of transformational One Page solutions.

Your clients will benefit by:

- Spending less time planning and more time implementing.
- Plans that are more effective because every user has a plan that is integrated with the total plan.
- Stronger communication between departments due to system's open-book structure.
- Better accountability using cloud-based Scorecards & Progress Reports.
- Shorter learning curve, focus is on performance & implementation, not learning software!

We Help Consultants Sell More Consulting!

We support your sales efforts with our professional sales training, fully functional demonstration system, and professional marketing collateral. You also benefit from our national branding efforts that include seven best-selling business planning books. Best of all, you will participate in an ongoing Advanced Practice Development Program designed to help consultants, advisors and coaches grow their practice!

Increase Sales and Profits with One Page Business Plan Engagements!

Our powerful tools can create spectacular breakthroughs in sales and profitability for your firm. Here are four of our popular offerings... serving four different market segments:

One Year Planning & Performance Management Programs for Management Teams -$50,000.
One Day Executive and Team Planning Retreats - $5,000.
1:1 Executive/Owner Business Plan Coaching - $3,000.
Interactive One Page Workshops and Webinars (per participant) - $895.

Find additional information about certification programs at our website: www.onepagebusinessplan.com

What One Page Consultants Are Saying...

Generated Over $250,000 the First Year

"The One Page Planning System has been incredibly profitable to our firm, generating over $250,000 in revenues in the first year. Over 20 clients have engaged us to implement it... they love the methodology!"
- Dr. Terry van der Werff, van der Werff Global Ltd., Hoover, AL

Our Project Fees Are Up Between 100% and 500% Across the Board

"Eighteen months ago, we re-engineered our 30 year-old sales training business which was losing margin and having a tough time competing in what had become a saturated, commodity marketplace. The One Page Business plan has helped turn our business into a high margin, differentiated, strategic sales & leadership consulting company. Our project fees are up between 100% and 500% across the board, and The One Page Business Plan has helped us add real, measurable value to our clients' businesses."
- Peter Krammer, ELA Sales, Inc., Napa, CA

A Versatile Process

"One Page Business Planning is a critical tool for all companies, regardless of size and stage of the business life cycle. It is a versatile process for leading your clients through the discovery of where they want to take their organizations, projects, territories, etc. Every management consultant should add One Page Business Planning to their practice."
- Anne L. Corell, Annapolis, MD

Sold Over 30 Significant One Page Business Plan Engagements

"For me, the One Page is not something I sell. I show it. People who get it and want to use it to transform their organizations are the people I want to work with. In the last three years I have sold over 30 significant One Page Business Plan engagements... it is the single most important tool in my consulting tool kit. I can't say enough about how helpful and supportive The One Page Business Plan Company has been to me. There is no question too stupid, no request too extreme or unusual, and no support too difficult for these folks. They have been great mentors, are strong friends and colleagues, and I count myself blessed to have them in my life."
- Skip Torresson, The Stewardship Group, Philadelphia, PA

Sold a $40,000 Consulting Engagement Within 4 Weeks

"I took the One Page Business Plan Certification program and four weeks later sold a $40,000 consulting engagement! The training was superb, and the follow-on assistance from everyone at The One Page Business Plan Company has been outstanding. I wish I had done this a long time ago! I would highly encourage you to add The One Page Business Plan to your toolkit!"
- Winston Copeland Jr, President, WWC Consulting, San Jose California

Great Training and Support!

"If you are looking for a great partnership in the world of business consulting, The One Page Business Plan is an excellent choice. I evaluated several options before choosing One Page Plans to be the backbone of my consulting practice. The training and support that I received in the first few months of becoming a licensee exceeded my expectations and continues to increase my value as a business consultant. The initial training was excellent, really top notch. I have had prior experiences with other systems, and I can honestly say that the program and partnership at The One Page Business Plan Company is the best!"
- Karen Kennedy, Founder & CEO Insights to Growth, Inc.

Learn more about upcoming certification programs at www.onepagebusinessplan.com

The 7 Hottest
Consulting Opportunities
with
The One Page Business Plan

1. **Managing the Strategic Plan:** All major corporations have strategic plans, however one of their biggest issues is the struggle with implementation and accountability. OPBP addresses this issue quickly, effectively at an attractive price point with the guidance and facilitation of a senior business coach.

2. **Blueprint for Growth:** Many companies hunkered down the last five years; they stayed in survival mode. Now they need to begin to rethink their business. Perfect application for OPBP.

3. **Sales Plans for High Performing Sales Professionals** (or those that want to be): One of the single largest usages of OPBP is with sales executives, managers and turbo charged sales professionals who want a simple, clear blueprint for immediate growth. One Page Plans do a great job of focusing these important people quickly... and they love OPBPs because they help them focus their time and energy on what will increase sales!

4. **Deferred Maintenance:** Business owners who want to sell their business are typically very disappointed when they receive their first valuation. It is not unusual for the valuation to be 10 – 20% of what they expected; many learn their business is not sellable. These owners learn that if they address the "deferred maintenance" they have ignored for the last few years they can expect a significant increase in their valuation. These owners are motivated to get a plan and execute it... but need assistance from an experienced advisor, business coach like you.

5. **Succession Planning:** 77 million Baby Boomers will be retiring over the next 10 years. Many of them own businesses and want to pass the business on to family members, partners, and associates. Unfortunately, too many of these people do not have the management and leadership skills necessary to run the business. A well-crafted one year OPBP program can move solid managers into executives with solid planning, execution, and performance management skills at a price substantially less than university prices. Also, our programs are private, practical, hands-on... and people actually learn and grow. But they must be implemented under the guidance and counsel of senior business coaches certified in The One Page Business Plan.

6. **Non-Profit Organizations:** We estimate 15,000 non-profit organizations use One Page Plans to manage all or part of their organizations. We have a specialty edition of The One Page Business Plan book and our cloud- based planning and performance management system just for non- profits. Many of non-profits refer to their One Page Business Plan as their One Page Promise. It focuses everyone on the team from Board members to frontline volunteers on achieving the organization's mission critical outcomes.

7. **Professional Development & Executive Leadership Programs:** One Page Business Plan books have been used by over 50 professors in a wide variety of undergraduate, graduate, and premium priced executive leadership programs. Many of our coaches and consultants incorporate OPBP curriculum, books and software into their professional development and executive development programs; these programs are designed to give upwardly mobile professionals, managers and executive the hard tools they need to successfully run their business units and companies.

Why Executives Invest in One Page Business Plans

(other than it simplifies planning!)

To Change Behavior...	They know they need to change behavior in order to achieve their most important goals and Vision. (my most favorite new question is to ask, "what behavior needs to change in your organization to achieve your most important goals... and your 3 – 5 year Vision?" I find most executives have NEVER been asked this question! They find it provocative and with a tiny bit of prompting have a solid answer. The OPBP program helps senior executives change behavior throughout the organization (even their own).
To Develop Effective Leaders	They need for stronger more effective leaders. Senior executives and business owners are looking for highly effective programs that strengthen strategic thinking, communication, decision making, execution and accountability... without having to spend 6 months in a classroom. They need programs to improve executive business and leadership skills while their executives, managers and team leaders are doing business!
To Cascade Strategic Decisions	They need a simple and effective way to cascade Strategic decisions made in the Boardroom throughout the entire organization.
To Increase Focus & Discipline	They need the next level of Focus and Discipline. Everywhere!
To Increase Sales	They need to increase sales by teaching their sales people how to think like a business owner! View their sales territory (role or responsibility) as a business.
To Develop New Executives	Business Leaders need to develop upwardly mobile professionals and managers to think, plan & execute like executives. This is a set of skills that takes time to master; the sooner they begin to develop these skills... the more valuable they are as an employee.

One Page Business Plans Grow People!

If you want to grow your business, you must grow your people.

Here's What Entrepreneurs, Business Owners and Executives are Saying about their One Page Plans...

"Putting together a 70-page business plan – replete with charts and graphs and spreadsheets – is a walk in the park. Getting it all right – exactly right – on a single page. Whoa! "Beautiful systems" are simple. One page business plan = the proverbial better mouse trap!"
Tom Peters
Best-Selling Business Author, Manchester Center, Vermont

"Using Point, Click, Plan! I had a solid draft of my plan within a couple of hours! After reviewing it with my team, they wrote plans w/ Point, Click, Plan! In a couple of days the entire team had solid plans ready for review and alignment. This is the new way to plan! No wasted time. Time previous spent on planning is now being spent on execution. We have procedures in place to revisit the plans quarterly, and we look forward to putting together next year's plan even quicker!"
America OnLine
Craig Peddie, Vice President and General Manager, Seattle, Washington

"We have found the web-based One Page Planning and Performance System valuable in managing our core business over the past two years. It provides a useful structure for our quarterly review meetings that helps us better focus on those things that make a real difference in our company!"
The Ken Blanchard Companies
Tom McKee, CEO, San Diego, California

"The One Page Planning method, along with the web-based tool, are great ways to help our managers stay strategic even though their days may be spent working primarily on tactical issues."
Herman Miller (San Francisco Franchise)
PJ Anderson, CEO, San Francisco, California

This is an innovative, fresh approach to business planning. If all loan applicants would provide us with clear, concise summaries of their business plan, a banker's life would be a lot easier.
Bank of Walnut Creek
Jim Ryan, Chairman and CEO, Walnut Creek, California

"We have used The One Page Business Plan with great success in the last two years! This web-based system will revolutionize and streamline our planning and performance management processes and improve our bottom-line results! The skills learned in writing a One Page Business Plan have helped bring a disciplined focus to our business.
Drake Beam Morin
Ken Kneisel, Executive Vice President, Atlanta, Georgia

"It's very easy for stockbrokers to get wrapped up in the market and lose perspective. In order to be successful for the long run, one must have a plan and The One Page Business Plan is a great tool."
Morgan Stanley Dean Witter
Ralph Miljanich, Vice President, Santa Cruz, California

"The One Page Business Plan is the business owner's Cliff Notes."
DaMert Company
Fred DaMert, Chairman, CEO & Chief Toy Maker, Berkeley, California

The One Page Business Plan Company

Workshops and TeleClasses

The One Page Business Plan® is available to you, your partners or team or your entire company as a workshop, annual retreat, teleclass or complete planning program. Experienced facilitators will tailor the presentation or facilitation to meet your needs.

All classes and programs are hands-on working sessions designed to teach participants how to write a clear, concise, understandable business plan, on a single page, in the quickest and simplest way possible.

Planning & Performance Management Software

This innovative web-based system uniquely links The One Page Business Plan with an executive dashboard and a simplified project tracking system. Over the last twelve years, companies from small professional service firms to international corporations have benefited from this system.

The system requires no IT support and can be learned in 30 minutes. Interested? The One Page Planning and Performance System is rapidly becoming the planning system of choice.

Professional Certification

We are interested in partnering with experienced business, government, and not-for-profit consultants and coaches. If your firm provides strategic planning and/or performance management consulting services, The One Page Business Plan may be a profitable addition to your toolkit.

Coaches and consultants who successfully complete the training and certification programs will be licensed to market and deliver One Page Business Plan products and services.

The One Page Business
Plan Company
1798 Fifth Street
Berkeley, CA 94710
Phone: (510) 705-8400
Fax: (510) 705-8403
jhoran@onepagebusinessplan.com
www.onepagebusinessplan.com

The One Page Business Plan...
Now a Best-Selling Series!

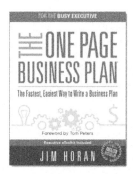

For the Busy Executive

Written specifically for professional business managers and executives. Thousands have already successfully written and implemented One Page Plans with this simple and effective planning methodology. Most of the hard work has already been done... so you'll never have to start with a blank page!

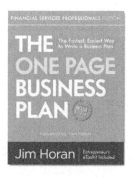

Financial Services Professionals Edition

Industry leaders in insurance, banking and financial services demanded we create this special edition for their industry. If you make your living selling financial products or services or managing people that do... this book was written for you!

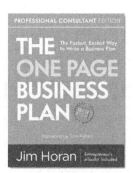

Professional Consultant Edition

New to consulting? Need to move your practice to the next level? This book was written by consultants, for consultants. It contains everything you need to create a blueprint for a successful consulting practice... all on a single page.

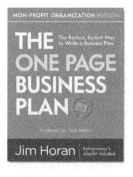

Non-Profit Organization Edition

If you are responsible for starting, managing or funding a non-profit... this book was written for you! One Page Plans create a community culture of discipline and accountability. This process helps executives, employees, volunteers and boards clearly define and live up to their promises.

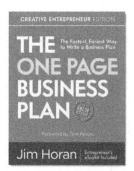

Creative Entrepreneur Edition

This is the million-dollar best seller that forever changed the way people write business plans. This is the fastest, easiest way for creative entreprenuers and small business owners to write a business plan!

Creative Entrepreneur Edition (Spanish version)

This is the Spanish language version of the million-dollar best seller that forever changed the way people write and implement business plans.

Available at www.onepagebusinessplan.com/books

Also on Amazon & other online retailers

The Professional Consultant's eToolkit

IMPORTANT:
Immediately after downloading and opening any of the eToolkit files we encourage you to save the file with a new name using the "SAVE AS" command in order to preserve the original content of the file.

No Technical Support
These eToolkit files are provided without technical or software support. Please refer to your Microsoft Word® or Excel® User Manuals for questions related to the use of these software programs. You may also use Google Docs... a free program from Google.

System Requirements:
Windows or Macintosh
Microsoft Word® and Excel® or Google Docs
No CD/ROM drive required

To download the files go to: www.onepagebusinessplan.com/cdpc

Made in the USA
Las Vegas, NV
24 May 2021